7

Show What You Know® on the
COMMON CORE

Assessing Student Knowledge of the Common Core State Standards (CCSS)

...ition

Mathematics

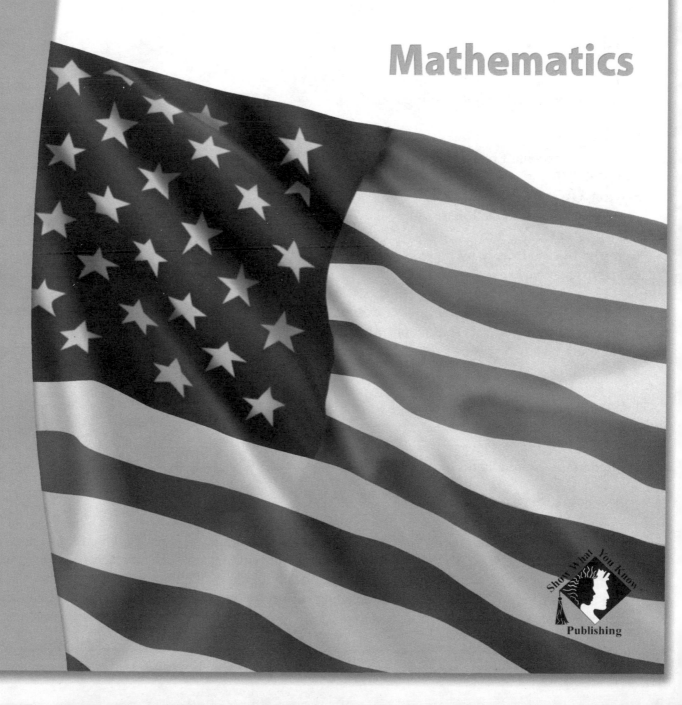

Show What You Know

Publishing

Published by:

Show What You Know® Publishing
www.showwhatyouknowpublishing.com

Distributed by:
Lorenz Educational Press, a Lorenz company
P.O. Box 802
Dayton, OH 45401-0802
www.LorenzEducationalPress.com

Standards are from the Common Core State Standards Initiative Web site at www.corestandards.org dated 2011.

Printed in the United States of America

ISBN: 978-1-5923-0463-9

Acknowledgements

Show What You Know® Publishing acknowledges the following for their efforts in making this assessment material available for students, parents, and teachers:

Cindi Englefield, President/Publisher
Eloise Boehm-Sasala, Vice President/Managing Editor
Jennifer Harney, Editor/Illustrator

About the Contributors

The content of this book was written BY teachers FOR teachers and students and was designed specifically for the Common Core State Standards for Grade 7 Mathematics. Contributions to the Mathematics section of this book were also made by the educational publishing staff at Show What You Know® Publishing. Dr. Jolie S. Brams, a clinical child and family psychologist, is the contributing author of the Test Anxiety and Test-Taking Strategies chapters of this book. Without the contributions of these people, this book would not be possible.

Table of Contents

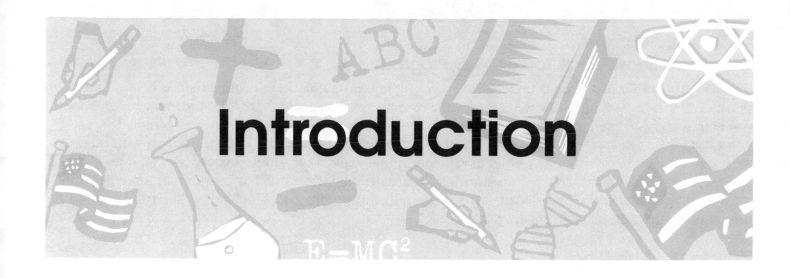

Introduction

Under the leadership of the National Governors Association (NGA) and the Council of Chief State School Officers (CCSSO), forty-eight states, two territories, and the District of Columbia have joined the Common Core State Standards Initiative (CCSSI) in 2009.

The CCSSI has produced Common Core State Standards to provide uniformity and high standards for student achievement in grades K–12 across the nation. These core standards provide a consistent, clear understanding of what students are expected to learn, so teachers and parents have a roadmap for what they need to do to help them. Further, these standards provide appropriate benchmarks for all students, regardless of where they live, and allow states to more effectively help all students to succeed.

To develop these standards, CCSSO and the NGA worked with representatives from participating states, a wide range of educators, content experts, researchers, national organizations, and community groups. The adopted core standards reflect the invaluable feedback from the general public, teachers, parents, business leaders, states, and content area experts.

As reflected in our *Show What You Know® on the Common Core* Student Workbooks and Parent/Teacher Editions for grades 3–8, Reading and Mathematics are the first subjects chosen for the Common Core State Standards because these two subjects are skills, upon which students build skill sets in other subject areas. They are also the subjects most frequently assessed for accountability purposes.

The *Show What You Know® on the Common Core* series for grades 3–8 is designed to review the new core standards and identify areas of students' strengths and needed improvement through diagnostic tests aligned to the core standards. In addition, the series provides chapters on test anxiety, test-taking strategies, and glossaries of terms for Reading and Mathematics to help prepare students with the knowledge and skills they need to succeed in the future.

Common Core State Standards will help ensure that students are receiving a high-quality education consistently, from school to school and state to state. These standards are a first step—a key building block—in providing students with a high-quality education that will prepare them for success in college and careers.

About the Show What You Know® Program

Show What You Know® Publishing has been developing test-preparation products since 1993. These products teach test-taking skills that are specific to state assessments and provide students with practice on full-length tests that simulate the format of state assessments. We understand that many students are not good test takers because they get nervous and may experience test anxiety. To help students with this issue, we provide a chapter, written by a child psychologist, that explains what test anxiety is, what it feels like, and ways to reduce the anxiety before, during, and after testing. Research has proven that three elements must exist for test success: knowledge, test-taking skills, and confidence. The Show What You Know® test-preparation program helps to ensure test success.

How to Use This Program

There are numerous ways to use the Student Workbook and Parent/Teacher Edition to help prepare your students for the Mathematics assessment. But before your students begin the assessments, take time to review the Test Anxiety and Test-Taking Strategies chapters in the Student Workbook to help them learn how to be better test takers. These important concepts can really improve students' test scores—it works!

Tips to Reduce Test Anxiety

You can read the entire chapter on test anxiety in the Student Workbook, or you can break it up into different sections, allowing yourself plenty of time to discuss and practice the methods suggested to reduce test stress. Identify what test anxiety is, and help students learn the symptoms. Explain to them that test anxiety is normal, and that there are ways it can be overcome. Tell them how being a little nervous will motivate them to do their best, but being very nervous could make them forget information they need to know for the test.

The rest of the Test Anxiety chapter offers activities to show ways to overcome test stress, such as thinking positively instead of negatively, emphasizing the importance of good physical health, and studying and practicing for the test. These are skills that will help your students succeed on state assessments, as well as other tests your students will face throughout their lives.

Test-Taking Strategies That Work!

The Test-Taking Strategies chapter can be used in a class discussion. The chapter gives specific test-taking strategies for state assessments. After reviewing the chapter, ask students if they have found ways to help them prepare for tests. Maybe they like to read stories with their parents or they make sure to get extra sleep the week of a test. All of these strategies can be used to help them do well on state assessments and other tests.

The Purpose of the Assessments

After you have walked your students through the Test Anxiety and Test-Taking Strategies chapters, students can take two 40-question assessments for Mathematics.

These tests were designed to simulate state assessments so that students can become familiar with the actual look of the test. The more familiar students are with the look of the test, the more confidence they will have when they take the actual assessment.

Correlation Charts Track Students' Strengths and Weaknesses

In this Parent/Teacher Edition, there are Correlation Charts for each Assessment. The standards as well as test item answers are listed for each question. To use the chart, write the students' names in the left-hand column. When students miss a question, place an "X" in the corresponding box. A column with a large number of "Xs" shows that your class needs more practice with that particular standard. You can quickly identify the needs of individual students.

Answer Key with Sample Responses

Answers to the Mathematics assessments are provided in the Parent/Teacher Edition. The correct answer is given, and for short-answer questions, a sample response is offered.

Additional Teaching Tools

A glossary of mathematics terms is provided in the Student Workbook to help your students understand terms that they should be familiar with in the seventh grade.

Suggested Timeline for Program Use

Now that you have a better understanding of how to use the Show What You Know® Test-Preparation Program, here is a suggested timeline for you to use to incorporate the program into your teaching schedule:

Suggested Timeline for Using the Show What You Know® on the Common Core for Grade 7 Mathematics, Student Workbook	
Week 1	Test Anxiety chapter
Week 2	Test-Taking Strategies chapter
Week 3	Review Glossary of Terms and Illustrations for Mathematics
Week 4	Mathematics Assessment One
Week 5	Additional Review After Results of Mathematics Assessment One
Week 6	Mathematics Assessment Two

Thank you for implementing the Show What You Know® Test-Preparation Program in your classroom. Good luck to you and all of your students as they prepare for their state assessment!

Test Anxiety

Introduction

The contents of the Test Anxiety chapter from the *Show What You Know® on the Common Core for Grade 7 Mathematics, Student Workbook*, begin on the next page. This chapter will help students begin to understand why they may feel some anxiety before taking a test. This anxiety is normal and is experienced by many people, not only students. The chapter offers information on different types of test takers and ideas on how to reduce worrisome feelings about tests.

Test Anxiety

What is Test Anxiety?

Test anxiety is just a fancy name for feeling nervous about tests. Everyone knows what it is like to be nervous. Feeling nervous is not a good experience.

Many students have anxiety about taking tests, so if you are a test worrier, don't let it worry you. Most likely, many of your fellow students and friends also have fearful feelings about tests but do not share these feelings with others. Seventh grade is a time when everyone wants to seem "grown up," and few seventh graders want to look weak or afraid in the eyes of their friends or their teachers. But not talking to others about anxiety only makes the situation worse. It makes you feel alone and also makes you wonder if there is something "wrong" with you. Be brave! Talk to your friends and teachers about test anxiety. You will feel better for sharing.

What Does It Feel Like to Have Test Anxiety?

Students who have test anxiety don't always feel the same way, but they always feel bad. Here are some ways that students feel when they are anxious about tests.

- **Students who have test anxiety rarely think good things about themselves.** They lack confidence in their abilities, and they are convinced they will do poorly on tests. Not only do they feel bad about themselves and their abilities, but they just can't keep negative thoughts out of their minds. They would probably make terrible detectives, because in spite of all the good things they could find out about themselves, they only think about what they can't do. And that's not the worst of it. Students with test anxiety also exaggerate. When they think of the smallest problem, it becomes a hundred times bigger, especially when they think about tests. They are very unforgiving of themselves. If they make a mistake, they always think the worst or exaggerate the situation. If they do poorly on a quiz, they never say, "Well, it's just a quiz, and I'll try better next time." Instead they think, "That test was terrible and I can only imagine how badly I'll do next week." For students with test anxiety, there is never a brighter day ahead. They don't think many good thoughts about themselves, and they certainly don't have a happy outlook on their lives.

- **Students who have test anxiety have poor "thinking habits."** Negative thinking is a habit just like any other habit. Some habits are good and some habits are bad, but negative thinking is probably the worst habit of all. A habit forms when you do something over and over again until it becomes so much a part of you that you don't think about it anymore. Students with test anxiety get into bad thinking habits. They develop negative ways of thinking about themselves and about schoolwork, especially about tests. They tend to make the worst out of situations and imagine all kinds of possibilities that probably will not happen. Their thoughts grow like a mushroom out of control. Besides having negative ideas about tests, they begin to have negative ideas about almost everything else in their lives. This is not a good way of thinking because the more negative they feel about themselves, the worse they do in school, and bad grades make them feel even worse about themselves. What a mess. Students who have constant negative thoughts about themselves and schoolwork probably have test anxiety.

Are You One of These "Test-Anxious" Seventh Graders?

As you have seen, students with test anxiety have negative thoughts about themselves, often feel anxious to the point of being ill, freak out and want to escape, and rarely show what they know on tests. Do any of the following kids remind you of yourself?

Stay-Away Stephanie

Stephanie's thoughts tell her it is better to stay away from challenges, especially tests. Stephanie is a good girl, but she is always in trouble at school for avoiding tests. Sometimes, she really feels ill and begs her mom to allow her to stay home on test days. At other times, Stephanie does anything to avoid school, refusing to get up in the morning or to leave the house to catch the bus. Stephanie truly believes there is nothing worse than taking a test. She is so overwhelmed with anxiety that she forgets about the problems that will happen when she stays away from her responsibilities. Unfortunately, the more she stays away, the worse the situation becomes. Stay-Away Stephanie feels less nervous when she doesn't face a test, but she never learns to face her fears.

Worried Wendy

Wendy is the type of seventh grader who always expects the worst thing to happen. She has many negative thoughts. Even when situations have turned out to be OK, Wendy focuses on the few bad things that happened. She exaggerates negative events and forgets about everything good. Her mind races a mile a minute with all sorts of thoughts and ideas about tests. The more she thinks, the worse she feels, and her problems become unbelievably huge. Instead of just worrying about a couple of difficult questions on a test, she finds herself thinking about failing the whole test, being made fun of by her friends, being grounded by her parents, and never going to college. She completely forgets that her parents would never be so strict, that her friends like her for many more reasons than her test grades, and that she has all sorts of career choices ahead of her. No one is going to hold it against her if she performed poorly on a test. It is not going to ruin her life. However, Wendy believes all of that would happen. Her negative thoughts get in the way of thinking anything positive.

- **Students who have test anxiety may feel physically uncomfortable or even ill.**

  It is important to know that your mind and body are connected. What goes on in your mind can change how your body feels, and how your body feels can influence what goes on in your thinking. When students have test anxiety, their thoughts might cause them to have physical symptoms which include a fast heartbeat, butterflies in the stomach, headaches, and all sorts of other physical problems. Some kids become so ill they end up going to the doctor because they believe they are truly sick. Some students miss a lot of school due to anxiety, but they aren't really ill. Instead, their thoughts are controlling their bodies in a negative way. Some anxious students do not realize that what they are feeling is anxiety. They miss many days of school, not because they are lazy or neglectful, but because they believe they are not feeling well. Unfortunately, the more school they miss, the more behind they are and the more nervous they feel. Students who suffer from test anxiety probably feel even worse on test days. Their uncomfortable physical feelings will make them either avoid the test completely or feel so bad during the test that they do poorly. Guess what happens then. They feel even worse about themselves, become more anxious, and the cycle goes on and on.

- **Students who have test anxiety "freak out" and want to escape.**

  Many students feel so bad when they are anxious that they will do anything to avoid that feeling. For most students, this means running away from problems, especially tests. Some students try to get away from tests by missing school. This does not solve any problems; the more a student is away from school, the harder schoolwork is, and the worse he or she feels. Some students worry about being worried. It may sound silly, but they are worried that they are going to freak out, and guess what happens . . . they do. They are so terrified that they will have uncontrollable anxious feelings that they actually get anxious feelings when thinking about this problem. For many students, anxiety is such a bad feeling that they will do anything not to feel anxious, even if it means failing tests or school. Although they know this will cause them problems in the future, their anxiety is so overwhelming they would rather avoid anxiety now and fail later. Unfortunately, this is usually what happens.

- **Students who have test anxiety do not show what they know on tests.**

  Students who have test anxiety do not make good decisions on tests. Instead of focusing their thoughts, planning out their answers, and using what they know, students find themselves "blanking out." They stare at the paper, and no answer is there. They become "stuck" and cannot move on. Some students come up with the wrong answers because their anxiety gets in the way of reading directions carefully and thinking about answers thoughtfully. Their minds are running in a hundred different ways and none of those ways seem to be getting them anywhere. They forget to use what they know, and they also forget to use study skills that can help students do their best. When students are so worried that they cannot make good decisions and use all of the talents they have, it is called test anxiety.

Critical Chris

Chris is the type of seventh grader who spends all of his time putting himself down. No matter what happens, he always feels he has been a failure. While some people hold grudges against others, Chris holds grudges against himself. No matter what little mistakes he makes, he can never forget them. Chris has had many good things happen to him in his life, and he has been successful many times. Unfortunately, Chris forgets all the good and only remembers the bad. Because he doesn't appreciate himself, Chris has test anxiety.

Victim Vince

Most seventh graders find it is important to take responsibility for their actions. It helps them understand that adulthood is just around the corner, and that they are smarter and more able than they ever thought they were. However, Vince is not like this. He can't take responsibility for himself at all. He thinks everything is someone else's fault and constantly complains about friends, parents, schoolwork, and especially tests. He tells himself, "They make those tests too hard." He sees the teachers as unfair, and he thinks life is generally against him. Vince does not feel there is anything he can do to help his situation, and there is little he thinks he can do to help himself with tests. Because he does not try to learn test-taking skills or to understand why he is afraid, he continues to feel hopeless and angry. Not surprisingly, he does poorly on tests, which only makes his thoughts about the world around him worse.

Perfect Pat

Everyone knows that there is more homework and responsibility in seventh grade than in previous grades. Everyone in the seventh grade needs to try his or her best, but no one should try as much as Pat does. All Pat does is worry. No matter what she does, it's never good enough. She will write book reports over and over and study for tests until she is exhausted. Trying hard is fine, but no matter what Pat does, she feels she has never done enough. Because she never accomplishes what she sets out to do (that would be impossible), she worries all the time. Her anxiety level gets higher and higher. The more anxious she becomes, the worse she does on tests. This just makes her study and worry more. What a terrible situation!

How Do I Handle Test Anxiety?

Test anxiety is a very powerful feeling that convinces students they are weak and helpless. Feelings of test anxiety can be so powerful it seems there is nothing you can do to stop them. Anxiety seems to take over your mind and body and leaves you feeling like you are going to lose the test anxiety battle for sure.

The good news is that there are many simple things you can do to win the battle over test anxiety. If you can learn these skills in the seventh grade, you are on the road to success in school and for all other challenges in your life.

- **Change the Way You Think.** Most of us don't "think about how we think." We just go along thinking our thoughts and never really consider whether they are helpful or not helpful or if they are right or wrong. We rarely realize how much the way we think has to do with how well we get along in life. Our thoughts can influence how we feel about ourselves, how we get along with other people, how well we do in school, and how we perform on tests.

- **The Soda Pop Test.** Most seventh graders have heard a parent or teacher tell them, "There is more than one side to any story." One student reported that his grandfather used to say, "There's more than one way to paint a fence." Have you ever considered how you think about different situations? Most situations can be looked at in many ways, both good and bad.

Take a can of soda pop and put it on your desk or dresser at home. Get out a piece of paper and a pen or a pencil. Now, draw a line down the middle of the paper. On one side, put a heading: "All the bad things about this can of soda pop." On the other side put another heading: "All the good things about this can of soda pop." If you think about that can of soda pop, you might come up with the following chart.

All the bad things about this can of soda pop	All the good things about this can of soda pop
Not an attractive color	Easy-to-read lettering
It's getting warm	Nice to have something to drink
Not much in the can	Inexpensive
Has a lot of sugar	Recyclable aluminum cans

Look how easy it is to write down good things or bad things about a silly can of soda pop. That can of soda pop is not really good or bad, it's just a can of soda pop, but we can either look at it in a positive way or we can think about everything negative that comes to our minds. Doesn't the same thing hold true for tests? Tests are not good or bad in themselves. Tests are just a way to challenge us and see what we know. Challenges can be stressful, but they can also be rewarding. Studying for tests can be boring and can take up a lot of free time, but we can also learn a lot and feel great about ourselves when we study. The way you think about tests will help determine how you do in a test-taking situation. Most importantly, how you feel about tests is related to your level of anxiety about test taking. Students who have negative thoughts and feelings about tests become anxious. Students who think positively are less anxious. To reduce test anxiety, try thinking about tests and testing situations using a positive frame of mind.

- **All or Nothing Thinking.**
  Nothing is ever as simple as it seems. Sometimes we convince ourselves something is going to be "awful" or "wonderful." Rarely does it turn out that way.

  Trouble comes along when students think tests are going to be an "awful" experience. If you dread something something happening, it is only going to make things worse. Also, you may be wrong. Nothing is as terrible as it seems. All the negative thoughts you have about the upcoming test cannot possibly be true. Thinking something is "awful" or "terrible" and nothing else only leads to trouble and failure. The more negative you feel about something, the worse things turn out.

  Very few things are "all good" or "all bad." This is especially true for tests. Recognizing the "bad" parts of tests can help you be successful. For example, the fact that you need to study for tests, to pay attention while you are taking tests, and to understand there are probably many more fun things to do in school than take tests are all "true" thoughts. "Good" thoughts are just as true, including the good feelings one gets from studying and the chance that you might do well. Having "all or nothing" thinking is going to get you nowhere. Successful and happy students know some experiences are better than others, but they try to look at a situation from all sides.

- **Mind Reading.**
  Some students believe they can read the minds of their parents and teachers. They assume if they do poorly on a test, everyone will think they are "dumb" or "lazy." The more their minds create all the terrible things that people may say about them, the more anxious they get. This just increases anxiety and definitely does not help students do well on tests.

- **Catastrophizing.**
  When people catastrophize, they make everything a catastrophe. A catastrophe is a disaster. It is when something terrible happens. When a student catastrophizes, his or her mind goes on and on creating terrible scenes of disasters. If someone put all these ideas into a movie script, the writer might be rich.

  Your state proficiency test is an important part of a seventh-grader's school year. It is a test that helps the student, the teacher, and the school. However, a seventh-grade student is much more than just his or her own personality, talents, and other successes in school. Each student is an individual who has his or her own great personality, talents, and other successes in school. If what people catastrophized about was really true, the whole world would be a terrible mess. Imagine if your mother cooked a dinner that didn't turn out quite right. This might mean everyone has to go out for fast food, but you wouldn't love your mother any less. It would be catastrophizing if your mother said, "Now that I burned the dinner, none of my kids will love me. They will probably just want to move out as quickly as they can, and my life will be ruined." Catastrophizing about a test is just as bad. Thinking that this test is going to be the worst experience of your life and that your future will be ruined will not help you feel comfortable when preparing for and taking the test.

- **Making "Should" Statements.**
  Students make themselves anxious when they think they "should" do everything. They feel they "should" be as smart as everyone else, "should" study more, and "should" not feel anxious about tests. All these thoughts are pretty ridiculous. You can't always be as smart as the next person, and you do not have to study until you drop to do well on tests. Instead of kicking yourself for not being perfect, it is better to think about all the good things you have done in your life. This will help you do better on tests and be happier in your life by reducing your anxiety.

How Do I Replace Worried Thoughts with Positive Ones?

As we have learned, there are all kinds of thoughts that make us anxious, such as feeling we "should" do everything, thinking we can read peoples' minds, catastrophizing, and thinking only bad thoughts about a situation. Learning how to stop these types of thoughts is very important. Understanding your thoughts and doing something about them help control test anxiety.

People who are worried or anxious can become happier when thinking positive thoughts. Even when situations are scary, such as a visit to the dentist, "positive imagery" is helpful. "Positive imagery" means thinking good thoughts to keep from thinking anxious thoughts. Positive and negative thoughts do not go together. If you are thinking something positive, it is almost impossible to think of something negative. Keep this in mind when test anxiety starts to become a bother.

Try these ideas the next time you find yourself becoming anxious.

- **Thoughts of Success.**
  Thinking "I can do it" thoughts can chase away thoughts of failure. Imagine times you were successful, such as when you performed well in a dance recital or figured out a complicated brain teaser. These are good things to think about. Telling yourself you have been successful in the past and can be successful in the future will chase away thoughts of anxiety.

- **Relaxing Thoughts.**
  Some people find that thinking calming or relaxing thoughts is helpful. Picturing a time in which you felt comfortable and happy can lessen your anxious feelings. Imagine yourself playing a baseball game, running through a park, or eating an ice cream cone; these are all positive thoughts that may get in the way of anxious ones. Some students find that listening to music on the morning of a test is helpful. It probably doesn't matter what music you listen to, as long as it makes you feel good about yourself, confident, and relaxed.

  Just as you can calm your mind, it is also important for you to relax your body. Practice relaxing your body. When students have test anxiety, their muscles become stiff. In fact, the whole body becomes tense. Taking deep breaths before a test and letting them out slowly as well as relaxing muscles in your body are all very helpful ways to feel less anxious. Your school counselors will probably have more ideas about relaxation. You may find that relaxation doesn't just help you on tests, but is helpful for other challenging situations and for feeling healthy overall.

- **Don't Let Yourself Feel Alone.**
  Everyone feels more anxious when they feel alone and separate from others. Talking to your friends, parents, and teachers about your feelings helps. Feeling anxious about tests does not mean there is something wrong with you. You will be surprised to find that many of your friends and fellow students also feel anxious about tests. You may be even more surprised to learn your parents and teachers have also had test anxiety. They know what you are going through and are there to support you.

- **Take Care of Yourself.**
  Everyone is busy. Many seventh graders are involved in all sorts of activities, including sports, music, and helping around the house. Often, you are so busy you forget to eat breakfast or you don't get enough sleep. Eating and sleeping right are important, especially before a test like your state proficiency test. If you are not a big breakfast eater, try to find something that you like to eat and get in the habit of eating breakfast. When you do not eat right, you may feel shaky and have a hard time concentrating, and your anxiety can increase. Being tired does not help either. Try to get in the habit of going to bed at a good time every night (especially the night before a test) so you can feel fresh, rested, and confident.

- **Practice Your Test-Taking Success.**
  People who have accomplished incredibly difficult goals have used their imaginations to help them achieve success. They thought about what they would do step by step to be successful.

  You can do the same. Think about yourself on the morning of the test. Imagine telling yourself positive thoughts and eating a good breakfast. Think about arriving at school and feeling confident that you will do fine on the test. Imagine closing your eyes before the test, breathing deeply, relaxing, and remembering all the study skills you have learned. The more you program your mind to think in a successful and positive way, the better off you will be.

- **Learn to Use Study Skills.**
  The next chapter in this book will help you learn test-taking strategies. The more you know about taking tests successfully, the calmer you will feel. Knowledge is power. Practice test-taking strategies to reduce your test anxiety.

- **Congratulate Yourself During the Test.**
  Instead of thinking, "I've only done five problems and I've got eight pages to go," or "I knew three answers were right but one mixed me up," reward yourself for what you have done. Tell yourself, "I got some answers right so far, so I bet I can do more." After all, if you don't compliment yourself, who will?

Conclusion

You are not alone if you feel stressed about tests. It is probably good to feel a little anxious, because it motivates you to do well. However, if you feel very anxious about tests, then reading, re-reading, and practicing the suggestions in this chapter will help you "tackle your test anxiety."

Test-Taking Strategies

Introduction

The contents of the Test-Taking Strategies chapter, from the *Show What You Know® on the Common Core for Grade 7 Mathematics, Student Workbook*, begin on the next page. This chapter will introduce students to test-taking strategies. These strategies are hints students can use for any test, but they are especially helpful for state assessments. This chapter will give students the tools they need to become successful test takers.

Test-Taking Strategies

Tools You Can Use on Tests Throughout Your Life!

Be An "Active Learner."

You can't learn anything by being a "sponge." Just because you are sitting in a pool of learning (your classroom) does not mean you are going to learn anything just by being there. Instead, students learn when they actively think and participate during the school day. Students who are active learners pay attention to what is being said. They also constantly ask themselves questions and their teachers questions about the subject. When able, they participate by making comments and joining discussions. Active learners enjoy school, learn more, feel good about themselves, and usually do better on tests. Remember the auto-repair mechanic? That person had a lot of knowledge about fixing cars. All the tools and strategies in the world will not help you unless you have benefited from what your teachers have tried to share.

Being an active learner takes time and practice. If you are the type of student who is easily bored or frustrated, it is going to take some practice to use your classroom time differently. Ask yourself the following questions.

- Am I looking at the teacher?
- Do I pay attention to what is being said?
- Do I have any questions or ideas about what the teacher is saying?
- Do I listen to what my fellow students are saying and think about their ideas?
- Do I work with others to try to solve difficult problems?
- Do I look at the clock and wonder what time school will be over, or do I appreciate what is happening during the school day and how much I can learn?
- Do I try to think about how my schoolwork might be helpful to me now or in the future?

Although you do need special tools and strategies to do well on tests, the more you learn, the better chance you have of doing well on tests. Think about Kristen.

There was a young girl named Kristen,
Who was bored and wouldn't listen.
She didn't train
To use her smart brain
And never knew what she was missing!

Test-Taking Strategies

All Students Can Do Their Best on Tests!

Most students want to do their best on tests. Tests are one important way for teachers to know how well students are doing and for students to understand how much progress they are making in their studies. Tests, like your state proficiency test, help schools measure how well students are learning so teachers and principals can make their schools even better. Students can do the best job possible in "showing what they know" by learning how to be good test takers.

It's just not possible to do a good job without the right tools. Test-taking strategies are tools to help you perform well on tests. Everyone needs good tools and strategies when facing a problem. If you do not have these, even the smartest or most talented person will do poorly. Think about people who are "wizards" at fixing cars and trucks. Your family's car "dies" in the middle of the road. The situation looks pretty hopeless. How are you ever going to get to that basketball game tomorrow if your parent's car is a mechanical mess? Suddenly, "magic" happens. The mechanic at the repair shop calls your parents and tells them the car is ready, just a day after it broke down. How did this happen? It happened because the auto-repair mechanic had a great deal of knowledge about cars. Most importantly, he had the right tools and strategies to fix the car. He knew how to look at the problem, and when he figured out what to do, he had some special gadgets to get the job done. You also can find special ways that will help you be a successful test taker.

When you think about a test or any other academic challenge, try to focus on what you can learn step by step and day by day. You will be surprised how all of this learning adds up to make you one of the smartest seventh graders ever. Think about Ray.

There was a smart boy named Ray,
Who learned something new every day.
He was pretty impressed
With what his mind could possess.
His excellent scores were his pay!

Get to Know the Test.
Most seventh graders are probably pretty used to riding in their parents' cars. They know how to make the air conditioning cooler or warmer, how to change the radio stations, and how to adjust the volume on the radio. Think about being a passenger in a totally unfamiliar car. You might think, "What are all those buttons? How do I even turn on the air conditioner? How do I make the window go up and down?" Now, think about taking your state proficiency test. Your state proficiency test is a test, but it may be different than some tests you have taken in the past. The more familiar you are with the types of questions on the test and how to record your answers, the better you will do. Working through the Mathematics chapter in this book will help you get to know the test. Becoming familiar with the test is a great test-taking tool. Think about Sue.

There was a kid named Sue,
Who thought her test looked new.
"I never saw this before!
How'd I get a bad score?"
If she practiced, she might have a clue!

Don't Depend on Luck.
Preparing for a test might feel stressful or boring at times, but it is an important part of learning how to show what you know and doing your best. Even the smartest student needs to spend time taking practice tests and listening to the advice of teachers about how to do well. Luck alone is not going to help you do well on tests. People who depend on luck do not take responsibility for themselves. Some people who believe in luck do not want to take the time and effort to do well. It is easier for them to say, "It's not my fault I did poorly. It's just not my lucky day." Some people just do not feel very good about their abilities. They get in the habit of saying, "Whatever happens will happen." They believe they can never do well no matter how much they practice or prepare. Students who feel they have no control over what happens to them usually have poor grades and do not feel very good about themselves.

Your performance on tests is not going to be controlled by luck. Instead, you can have a lot of control over how well you do in many areas of your life, including test taking. Don't be like Chuck.

There was a cool boy named Chuck.
Who thought taking tests was just luck.
He never prepared.
He said, "I'm not scared."
When his test scores appear, he should duck!

Do Your Best Every Day.
Many students find seventh grade much different than other grades. Suddenly, the work seems really hard. Not only that, but your teachers are no longer treating you like a baby. That's good in some ways, because it gives you more freedom and responsibility, but there sure is a lot to learn. You might feel the same way about tests; you may feel you'll never be prepared. Many times when we are faced with new challenges, it is easy just to give up.

Students are surprised when they find that if they just set small goals for themselves, they can learn an amazing amount. If you learn just one new fact every day of the year, at the end of the year, you will know 365 new facts. You could use those to impress your friends and family. Now think about what would happen if you learned three new facts every day. At the end of the year, you would have learned 1,095 new facts. Soon you will be on your way to having a mind like an encyclopedia.

Read Directions and Questions Carefully!
One of the worst mistakes a student can make on a test is to ignore directions or to read questions carelessly. By the time some students are in the seventh grade, they think they have heard every direction or question ever invented, and it is easy for them to "tune out" directions. Telling yourself, "These directions are just like other directions," or "I'm not really going to take time to read this question because I know what the question will be," are not good test-taking strategies. It is impossible to do well on any test without knowing what is being asked.

Reading directions and questions slowly, repeating them to yourself, and asking yourself if what you are reading makes sense are powerful test-taking strategies. Think about Fred.

There was a nice boy named Fred,
Who ignored almost all that he read.
The directions were easy,
But he said, "I don't need these!"
He should have read them instead.

Know How to Fill in Those Answer Bubbles!
Most seventh graders have taken tests that ask them to fill in answer bubbles. You might be a very bright seventh grader, but you will never "show what you know" unless you fill in the answer bubbles correctly. Don't forget: a computer will be "reading" your multiple-choice question answers. If you do not fill in the answer bubble darkly or if you use a check mark or dot instead of a dark mark, your smart thinking will not be counted. Look at the examples given below.

Correct

Incorrect

Practice Here

Learning how to fill in answer bubbles takes practice, practice, and more practice. It may not be how you are used to answering multiple-choice questions, but it is the only way to give a right answer on your state proficiency test. Think about Kay!

A stubborn girl named Kay,
Liked to answer questions her own way.
So her marked answer bubbles,
Gave her all sorts of troubles,
Her test scores ruined her day!

Speeding Through the Test Doesn't Help.
Most students have more than enough time to read and answer all the questions on a test. There will always be some students who finish the test more quickly than others, but this does not mean the test was easier for them or their answers are correct. Whether you finish at a faster rate or at a slower rate than other students in your class is not important. As long as you take your time, are well prepared, concentrate on the test, and use some of the skills in this book, you should be able to do just fine. You will not get a better score just because you finish the test before everyone else. Speeding through a test item or through a whole test does not help you do well. In fact, students do their best when they work at a medium rate of speed, not too slow and not too fast. Students who work too slowly tend to get worried about their answers and sometimes change correct answers into incorrect ones. Students who work too fast often make careless mistakes, and many of them do not read directions or questions carefully. Think about Liz.

There was a seventh grader named Liz,
Who sped through her test like a whiz,
She thought she should race
At a very fast pace,
But it caused her to mess up her quiz.

Remember, it is fine to write in your test booklet. Think about Dwight.

There was a smart kid named Dwight,
Who marked answers that looked to be right.
He'd put a plus sign
Or a dash or a line.
Now the whole world knows he is bright!

- **Use what you know to "power guess."**

Not everything you know was learned in a classroom. Part of what you know comes from just living your life. When you take a test, you should use everything you have learned in school, but you should also use your experiences outside the classroom to help you answer questions correctly. Using your "common sense," as well as other information you know, will help you do especially well on a test. Try to use what you know from the world around you to eliminate obviously wrong answers. If you can rule out just one answer that you are certain is not correct, you are going to greatly increase your chances of guessing another answer correctly. For example, if you are given a question in which you are asked to find the square footage of a home, and one of the answers seems very small, you might be able to count that answer out using your own experiences. Although the mathematics might be difficult for you, your common sense has eliminated one likely wrong answer. Think about Drew.

There was a boy named Drew,
Who forgot to use what he knew.
He had lots of knowledge,
He could have been in college!
But his right answers were few.

Answer Every Question.

There is no reason that you should not attempt to answer every question you encounter on a test. Even if you don't know the answer, there are ways for you to increase your chances of choosing the correct response. Use the helpful strategies described below to help you answer every question to the best of your ability.

- **If you don't know the answer, guess.**

Did you know that on your state proficiency test there is no penalty for guessing? That is really good news. That means you have a one out of four chance of getting a multiple-choice question right, even if you just close your eyes and guess. That means that for every four questions you guess, you should get about 25% (1 out of 4) of the questions right. Guessing alone is not going to make you a star on the test, but leaving multiple-choice items blank is not going to help you either.

Now comes the exciting part. If you can rule out one of the four answer choices, your chances of answering correctly are now one out of three. You can almost see your test score improving right before your eyes.

Although it is always better to be prepared for the test and to study in school, we all have to guess at one time or another. Some of us do not like to guess because we are afraid of choosing the wrong answer, but on a test, it is better to guess than leave an answer blank. Think about Jess.

There was a smart girl named Jess,
Who thought it was useless to guess.
If a question was tough,
She just gave up.
This only added to her stress.

- **Use a "code" to help you make good guesses.**

Some students use a "code" to rate each answer when they feel they might have to guess. Using your pencil in the test booklet, you can mark the following codes next to each multiple-choice response so you can make the best possible guess. The codes are as follows:

(+) Putting a "plus sign" by your answer means you are not sure if this answer is correct, but you think this answer is probably more correct than the others.

(?) Putting a "question mark" by your answer means you are unsure if this is the correct answer, but you don't want to rule it out completely.

(−) Putting a "minus sign" by your answer means you are pretty sure this is the wrong answer. You should then choose from the other answers to make an educated guess.

- **Do Not Get Stuck on One Question.**

One of the worst things you can do on a test is to get stuck on one question. Your state proficiency test gives you many chances to show all that you have learned. Not knowing the answer to one or two questions is not going to hurt your test results very much.

When you become stuck on a question, your mind plays tricks on you. You begin to think that you are a total failure, and your worries become greater and greater. This worrying gets in the way of your doing well on the rest of the test. Remember, very few students know all the answers on a test. If you are not sure of the answer after spending some time on it, mark it in your test booklet and come back to it later. When you come back to that question later, you might find a new way of thinking. Sometimes, another question or answer later in the test will remind you of a possible answer to the question that had seemed difficult. If not, you can use your guessing strategies to solve the questions you are unsure of after you have answered all the questions you know. Also, when you move on from a troubling question and find you are able to answer other questions correctly, you will feel much better about yourself and you will feel calmer. This will help you have a better chance of succeeding on a question that made you feel "stuck." Think about Von.

There was a sweet girl named Von.
Who got stuck and just couldn't go on.
She'd sit there and stare,
But the answer wasn't there.
Before she knew it, all the time was gone.

- **Always, and This Means Always, Recheck Your Work.**

Everyone makes mistakes. People make the most mistakes when they feel a little worried or rushed. Checking your work is a very important part of doing your best. This is particularly true in the Mathematics section, where careless mistakes can lead to a wrong answer, even when you used the right steps. Going back and rechecking your work is very important. In the Mathematics section, look at your calculations to make sure that you did not mistake one number for another and that you lined up your calculations neatly and legibly. If any numbers seem messy or unreadable, you might want to recheck your calculations. If an answer does not seem to make sense, go back and reread the question, or recheck your work. Think about Jen.

There was a quick girl named Jen.
Who read stuff once and never again.
It would have been nice
If she'd reread it twice.
Her test scores would be better then!

- **Pay Attention to Yourself and Not Others.**

It is easy to look around the room and wonder how friends are doing. However, it is important to think about how you are using tools and strategies. Don't become distracted by friends. You are going to waste a lot of time if you try to figure out what your friends are doing. Instead, use that time to "show what you know."

If it becomes hard for you to pay attention, give yourself a little break. If you feel you are getting a little tense or worried, or if a question seems tough, close your eyes for a second or two. Think positive thoughts. Try to put negative thoughts out of your mind. You might want to stretch your arms or feet or move around a little to help you focus. Anything you may do to help pay better attention to the test is a great test-taking strategy. Think about Kirk.

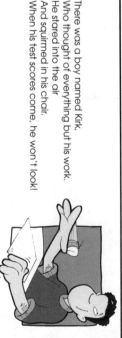

There was a boy named Kirk.
Who thought of everything but his work.
He stared into the air
And squirmed in his chair,
When his test scores come, he won't look!

General Test-Taking Strategies for Mathematics

The Mathematics Assessment will ask you to answer multiple-choice questions and short-answer questions. Here are some good strategies to use on the Mathematics Assessment.

- **Neatness Counts.**

Numbers that no one can read, or that are out of place, may hurt your score. For short-answer questions and completion items, write your answer clearly in the space provided. For multiple-choice answers, make sure you fill in the answer circle completely.

- **Rechecking Your Work is Important.**

Always recheck your answers to math problems. Rechecking problems may be very helpful if you have time left at the end of the test.

- **You Can Draw a Table, Chart, or Picture to Help You Answer the Question.**

Diagramming or drawing what you already know can help you find the right answer.

Consider this example:

1   Marcus and his three friends are looking for a snack. They find five different types of ice cream: chocolate chip, fudge ripple, strawberry, vanilla, and orange sherbet in the freezer and five different cookies: chocolate chip, sugar, peanut butter, raisin, and oatmeal in the cookie jar. For each flavor of ice cream there is only enough for one serving, and only one cookie of each kind.

After his friends have made their choices, how many types of ice cream and cookies are left for Marcus to choose from?

A. 2 types of ice cream and 1 type of cookie

B. 2 types of ice cream and 2 types of cookies

C. 1 type of ice cream and 2 types of cookies

D. 1 type of ice cream and 1 type of cookie

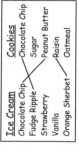

Ice Cream	Cookies
Chocolate Chip	Chocolate Chip
Fudge Ripple	Sugar
Strawberry	Peanut Butter
Vanilla	Raisin
Orange Sherbet	Oatmeal

By creating a diagram, you can see there are 2 types of ice cream and 2 types of cookies left for Marcus to choose from. Choice B is correct.

Specific Strategies for Online Tests

Kids usually have two different kinds of thoughts about taking a test on a computer. Some say, "Well, I use my computer all the time … I'm not going to even pay attention to the test … computers are easy!" Some kids think in the opposite way. They say, "A computer test? That has to be even scarier than a regular test … there is no way I am going to do well!" The truth is that both of them are wrong. You have to use some special strategies to do your best on computer tests, and when you do, you will do your best!

1.   **Read the Directions!** Here is a silly question: Would you want to eat a cake your friend made if he didn't read the directions on the box? Probably not! But even if you aren't a famous cook, you could make a pretty good cake if you read and follow directions. If you read the directions for EACH QUESTION you will have a much better chance of showing what you know. Because even if you know a lot, you have to answer what the question asks. Don't leave out this important step to test success!

2.   **Don't Go With the First Answer.** Take a little time and read the WHOLE question and read the WHOLE question and ALL the answer choices. The first answer that looks right is not always the best. Think about going out to dinner with your grandmother. You look at the menu and see "Big Ole Burger"! That sounds good. But if you looked at ALL the menu choices, you might have found your favorite tacos! The burger was good, but if you took more time, you would have found a better choice.

3.   **Ask Yourself … How Much Time Do I Have?** You will have a certain amount of time to complete each section of the test. Always check to see how much time you will have. Practice also helps. Did you know that football players practice and practice to see how long it takes to line up and start a play? After a while they are more relaxed and don't worry about time running out. You need to take some practice tests to feel comfortable with timed tests.

4.   **Is There a Good Way to Guess?** Most of the time it is a good idea to guess, especially if you can make an "educated" guess! That means you know some things about the question, but not everything. Let's say you aren't quite sure where your cousin lives, but you know it is cold and snows there all the time. One of your friends says that maybe your cousin lives in Georgia. You don't think that is right, because it hardly gets very cold there, and it is right next to Florida! So you can make an "educated guess" that "Georgia" isn't the right answer!

5. **When Should You Guess?** Unless the directions say that you will lose points for guessing, go for it! Educated guesses are the best, but even if you are really unsure of the answer, calm down and take a guess. If you have four possible answers, and make a guess, you have a one out of four chance of guessing correctly. That is like having three old pennies and one new penny in a bowl. If you just reach in, you will get the new penny one out of every four times you try. That's why you should answer every question!

6. **Don't Mess With That Test Window!** When people get a little nervous, they tend to make silly mistakes. One kid was rushing to make some toast before rushing off to school, and he unplugged the toaster instead of making the toast! Figure out how the computer screen works, and DON'T close that test window!

7. **Have a Good Attitude!** The better you feel, the better you will do! Remind yourself of how much you have learned in school. Remember that while this test is important, your teachers will still like you a lot no matter how you do. Just do your best and feel good about yourself. Did you know that when runners have a good attitude, that they win more often? Well, the same goes for you and tests!

8. **If You Have Time Left, Use It!** You can use extra time to help you do your best! If your computer test allows, review your answers, especially if you guessed on a question or two. Take a deep breath and calm down. You might find that a better answer comes into your mind. Talk to yourself a little about some of your answers. You might ask yourself, "I chose the answer that said that it will take 6 hours for that ice cube to melt. That seems like a long time … maybe I better recheck this and see if that makes sense."

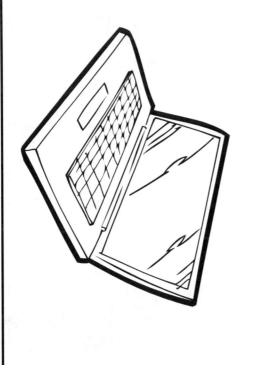

Seventh graders all over have good ideas about tests. Here are some of them!

- Ask yourself, "Did I answer the question that was asked?" Carefully read the question so you can give the right answer.

- Read each answer choice before filling in an answer bubble. Sometimes, you read the first choice, and it seems right. But, when you get to the third choice, you realize that's the correct answer. If you had stopped with the first choice, you would have answered the question incorrectly. It is important to read all four choices before answering the question.

- Remember, nobody is trying to trick you. Do not look for trick answers. There will always be a right answer. If the answer choices do not look right, mark the question and go back to it later.

- Don't look around the room. Don't worry about how fast your friends are working, and don't worry about how well they are doing. Only worry about yourself. If you do that, you will do better on the test.

Mathematics

Introduction

The Mathematics assessment reflects what students should know and should be able to do in the seventh grade. State assessments assess students' knowledge with multiple-choice and constructed-response items. The questions are not meant to confuse or trick them but are written so students have the best opportunity to show what they know about mathematics.

The Mathematics chapter in the *Show What You Know® on the Common Core for Grade 7 Mathematics, Parent/Teacher Edition,* contains the following:

- The Common Core State Standards for Grade 7.

- Two full-length Mathematics Assessments from the Student Workbook, in reduced-page format, with sample responses, correlation charts, a standards checklist, and a grading document.

Ratios and Proportional Relationships   7.RP

Analyze proportional relationships and use them to solve real-world and mathematical problems.

1. Compute unit rates associated with ratios of fractions, including ratios of lengths, areas and other quantities measured in like or different units. *For example, if a person walks $\frac{1}{2}$ mile in each $\frac{1}{4}$ hour, compute the unit rate as the complex fraction $\frac{1}{2} / \frac{1}{4}$ miles per hour, equivalently 2 miles per hour.*

2. Recognize and represent proportional relationships between quantities.

    a. Decide whether two quantities are in a proportional relationship, e.g., by testing for equivalent ratios in a table or graphing on a coordinate plane and observing whether the graph is a straight line through the origin.

    b. Identify the constant of proportionality (unit rate) in tables, graphs, equations, diagrams, and verbal descriptions of proportional relationships.

    c. Represent proportional relationships by equations. *For example, if total cost t is proportional to the number n of items purchased at a constant price p, the relationship between the total cost and the number of items can be expressed as t = pn.*

    d. Explain what a point (x, y) on the graph of a proportional relationship means in terms of the situation, with special attention to the points $(0, 0)$ and $(1, r)$ where r is the unit rate.

3. Use proportional relationships to solve multistep ratio and percent problems. *Examples: simple interest, tax, markups and markdowns, gratuities and commissions, fees, percent increase and decrease, percent error.*

The Number System   7.NS

Apply and extend previous understandings of operations with fractions to add, subtract, multiply, and divide rational numbers.

1. Apply and extend previous understandings of addition and subtraction to add and subtract rational numbers; represent addition and subtraction on a horizontal or vertical number line diagram.

    a. Describe situations in which opposite quantities combine to make 0. *For example, a hydrogen atom has 0 charge because its two constituents are oppositely charged.*

    b. Understand $p + q$ as the number located a distance $|q|$ from p, in the positive or negative direction depending on whether q is positive or negative. Show that a number and its opposite have a sum of 0 (are additive inverses). Interpret sums of rational numbers by describing real-world contexts.

    c. Understand subtraction of rational numbers as adding the additive inverse, $p - q = p + (-q)$. Show that the distance between two rational numbers on the number line is the absolute value of their difference, and apply this principle in real-world contexts.

    d. Apply properties of operations as strategies to add and subtract rational numbers.

2. Apply and extend previous understandings of multiplication and division and of fractions to multiply and divide rational numbers.

   a. Understand that multiplication is extended from fractions to rational numbers by requiring that operations continue to satisfy the properties of operations, particularly the distributive property, leading to products such as $(-1)(-1) = 1$ and the rules for multiplying signed numbers. Interpret products of rational numbers by describing real-world contexts.

   b. Understand that integers can be divided, provided that the divisor is not zero, and every quotient of integers (with non-zero divisor) is a rational number. If p and q are integers, then $-(p/q) = (-p)/q = p/(-q)$. Interpret quotients of rational numbers by describing real-world contexts.

   c. Apply properties of operations as strategies to multiply and divide rational numbers.

   d. Convert a rational number to a decimal using long division; know that the decimal form of a rational number terminates in 0s or eventually repeats.

3. Solve real-world and mathematical problems involving the four operations with rational numbers. *(Computations with rational numbers extend the rules for manipulating fractions to complex fractions.)*

Expressions and Equations   7.EE

Use properties of operations to generate equivalent expressions.

1. Apply properties of operations as strategies to add, subtract, factor, and expand linear expressions with rational coefficients.

2. Understand that rewriting an expression in different forms in a problem context can shed light on the problem and how the quantities in it are related. *For example, a + 0.05a = 1.05a means that "increase by 5%" is the same as "multiply by 1.05."*

Solve real-life and mathematical problems using numerical and algebraic expressions and equations.

3. Solve multi-step real-life and mathematical problems posed with positive and negative rational numbers in any form (whole numbers, fractions, and decimals), using tools strategically. Apply properties of operations to calculate with numbers in any form; convert between forms as appropriate; and assess the reasonableness of answers using mental computation and estimation strategies. *For example: If a woman making $25 an hour gets a 10% raise, she will make an additional 1/10 of her salary an hour, or $2.50, for a new salary of $27.50. If you want to place a towel bar 9 3/4 inches long in the center of a door that is 27 1/2 inches wide, you will need to place the bar about 9 inches from each edge; this estimate can be used as a check on the exact computation.*

4. Use variables to represent quantities in a real-world or mathematical problem, and construct simple equations and inequalities to solve problems by reasoning about the quantities.

    a. Solve word problems leading to equations of the form $px + q = r$ and $p(x + q) = r$, where p, q, and r are specific rational numbers. Solve equations of these forms fluently. Compare an algebraic solution to an arithmetic solution, identifying the sequence of the operations used in each approach. *For example, the perimeter of a rectangle is 54 cm. Its length is 6 cm. What is its width?*

    b. Solve word problems leading to inequalities of the form $px + q > r$ or $px + q < r$, where p, q, and r are specific rational numbers. Graph the solution set of the inequality and interpret it in the context of the problem. *For example: As a salesperson, you are paid $50 per week plus $3 per sale. This week you want your pay to be at least $100. Write an inequality for the number of sales you need to make, and describe the solutions.*

Geometry   7.G

Draw, construct, and describe geometrical figures and describe the relationships between them.

1. Solve problems involving scale drawings of geometric figures, including computing actual lengths and areas from a scale drawing and reproducing a scale drawing at a different scale.

2. Draw (freehand, with ruler and protractor, and with technology) geometric shapes with given conditions. Focus on constructing triangles from three measures of angles or sides, noticing when the conditions determine a unique triangle, more than one triangle, or no triangle.

3. Describe the two-dimensional figures that result from slicing three-dimensional figures, as in plane sections of right rectangular prisms and right rectangular pyramids.

Solve real-life and mathematical problems involving angle measure, area, surface area, and volume.

4. Know the formulas for the area and circumference of a circle and use them to solve problems; give an informal derivation of the relationship between the circumference and area of a circle.

5. Use facts about supplementary, complementary, vertical, and adjacent angles in a multi-step problem to write and solve simple equations for an unknown angle in a figure.

6. Solve real-world and mathematical problems involving area, volume, and surface area of two- and three-dimensional objects composed of triangles, quadrilaterals, polygons, cubes, and right prisms.

Statistics and Probability   7.SP

Use random sampling to draw inferences about a population.

1. Understand that statistics can be used to gain information about a population by examining a sample of the population; generalizations about a population from a sample are valid only if the sample is representative of that population. Understand that random sampling tends to produce representative samples and support valid inferences.

2. Use data from a random sample to draw inferences about a population with an unknown characteristic of interest. Generate multiple samples (or simulated samples) of the same size to gauge the variation in estimates or predictions. *For example, estimate the mean word length in a book by randomly sampling words from the book; predict the winner of a school election based on randomly sampled survey data. Gauge how far off the estimate or prediction might be.*

Draw informal comparative inferences about two populations.

3. Informally assess the degree of visual overlap of two numerical data distributions with similar variabilities, measuring the difference between the centers by expressing it as a multiple of a measure of variability. *For example, the mean height of players on the basketball team is 10 cm greater than the mean height of players on the soccer team, about twice the variability (mean absolute deviation) on either team; on a dot plot, the separation between the two distributions of heights is noticeable.*

4. Use measures of center and measures of variability for numerical data from random samples to draw informal comparative inferences about two populations. *For example, decide whether the words in a chapter of a seventh-grade science book are generally longer than the words in a chapter of a fourth-grade science book.*

Investigate chance processes and develop, use, and evaluate probability models.

5. Understand that the probability of a chance event is a number between 0 and 1 that expresses the likelihood of the event occurring. Larger numbers indicate greater likelihood. A probability near 0 indicates an unlikely event, a probability around 1/2 indicates an event that is neither unlikely nor likely, and a probability near 1 indicates a likely event.

6. Approximate the probability of a chance event by collecting data on the chance process that produces it and observing its long-run relative frequency, and predict the approximate relative frequency given the probability. *For example, when rolling a number cube 600 times, predict that a 3 or 6 would be rolled roughly 200 times, but probably not exactly 200 times.*

7. Develop a probability model and use it to find probabilities of events. Compare probabilities from a model to observed frequencies; if the agreement is not good, explain possible sources of the discrepancy.

   a. Develop a uniform probability model by assigning equal probability to all outcomes, and use the model to determine probabilities of events. *For example, if a student is selected at random from a class, find the probability that Jane will be selected and the probability that a girl will be selected.*

   b. Develop a probability model (which may not be uniform) by observing frequencies in data generated from a chance process. *For example, find the approximate probability that a spinning penny will land heads up or that a tossed paper cup will land open-end down. Do the outcomes for the spinning penny appear to be equally likely based on the observed frequencies?*

8. Find probabilities of compound events using organized lists, tables, tree diagrams, and simulation.

   a. Understand that, just as with simple events, the probability of a compound event is the fraction of outcomes in the sample space for which the compound event occurs.

   b. Represent sample spaces for compound events using methods such as organized lists, tables, and tree diagrams. For an event described in everyday language (e.g., "rolling double sixes"), identify the outcomes in the sample space which compose the event.

   c. Design and use a simulation to generate frequencies for compound events. *For example, use random digits as a simulation tool to approximate the answer to the question: If 40% of donors have type A blood, what is the probability that it will take at least 4 donors to find one with type A blood?*

Glossary

addend: Numbers added together to give a sum. For example, 2 + 7 = 9. The numbers 2 and 7 are addends.

addition: An operation joining two or more sets where the result is the whole.

a.m.: The hours from midnight to noon; from Latin words *ante meridiem* meaning "before noon."

analyze: To break down information into parts so that it may be more easily understood.

angle: A figure formed by two rays that meet at the same end point called a vertex. Angles can be obtuse, acute, right, or straight.

area: The number of square units needed to cover a region. The most common abbreviation for area is *A*.

Associative Property of Addition: The grouping of addends can be changed and the sum will be the same.
Example: (3 + 1) + 2 = 6; 3 + (1 + 2) = 6.

Associative Property of Multiplication: The grouping of factors can be changed and the product will be the same.
Example: (3 x 2) x 4 = 24; 3 x (2 x 4) = 24.

attribute: A characteristic or distinctive feature.

average: A number found by adding two or more quantities together and then dividing the sum by the number of quantities. For example, in the set {9, 5, 4}, the average is 6: 9 + 5 + 4 = 18; 18 ÷ 3 = 6. *See mean.*

axes: Plural of axis. Perpendicular lines used as reference lines in a coordinate system or graph; traditionally, the horizontal axis (*x*-axis) represents the independent variable and the vertical axis (*y*-axis) represents the dependent variable.

bar graph: A graph using bars to show data.

capacity: The amount an object holds when filled.

chart: A way to show information, such as in a graph or table.

circle: A closed, curved line made up of points that are all the same distance from a point inside called the center.
Example: A circle with center point *P* is shown below.

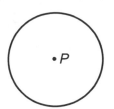

circle graph: Sometimes called a pie chart; a way of representing data that shows the fractional part or percentage of an overall set as an appropriately-sized wedge of a circle.
Example:

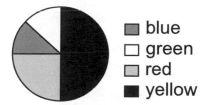

■ blue
□ green
▨ red
■ yellow

circumference: The boundary line or perimeter of a circle; also, the length of the perimeter of a circle.
Example:

Commutative Property of Addition: Numbers can be added in any order and the sum will be the same.
Example: 3 + 4 = 4 + 3.

Commutative Property of Multiplication: Numbers can be multiplied in any order and the product will be the same.
Example: 3 x 6 = 6 x 3.

compare: To look for similarities and differences. For example, is one number greater than, less than, or equal to another number?

conclusion: A statement that follows logically from other facts.

Glossary

cone: A solid figure with a circle as its base and a curved surface that meets at a point.

cones

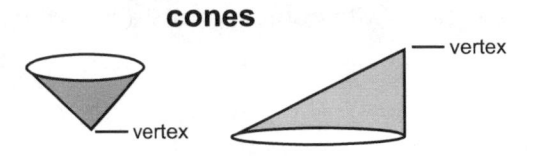

congruent figures: Figures that have the same shape and size.

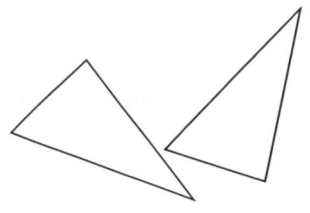

congruent triangles

cube: A solid figure with six faces that are congruent (equal) squares.

cylinder: A solid figure with two circular bases that are congruent (equal) and parallel to each other connected by a curved lateral surface.

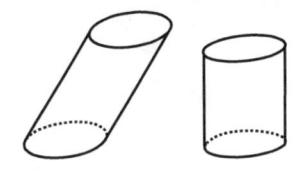

data: Information that is collected.

decimal number: A number expressed in base 10, such as 39.456, where each digit's value is determined by multiplying it by some power of 10.

denominator: The bottom number in a fraction.

diagram: A drawing that represents a mathematical situation.

difference: The answer when subtracting two numbers.

distance: The amount of space between two points.

dividend: A number in a division problem that is divided. Dividend ÷ divisor = quotient.
Example: In 15 ÷ 3 = 5, 15 is the dividend.

$$\text{divisor}\overline{)\text{dividend}}^{\text{quotient}} \qquad 3\overline{)15}^{\;5}$$

divisible: A number that can be divided by another number without leaving a remainder. Example: 12 is divisible by 3 because 12 ÷ 3 is an integer, namely 4.

division: An operation that tells how many equal groups there are or how many are in each group.

divisor: The number by which another number is divided. Example: In 15 ÷ 3 = 5, 3 is the divisor.

$$\text{divisor}\overline{)\text{dividend}}^{\text{quotient}} \qquad 3\overline{)15}^{\;5}$$

edge: The line segment where two faces of a solid figure meet.

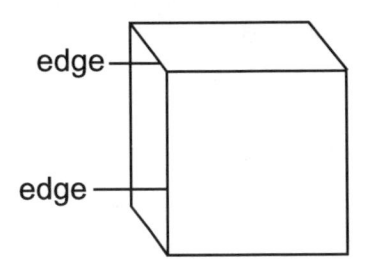

equivalent fractions: Two fractions with equal values.

equality: Two or more sets of values that are equal.

equation: A number sentence that says two expressions are equal (=). Example: 4 + 8 = 6 + 6.

estimate: To find an approximate value or measurement of something without exact calculation.

even number: A whole number that has a 0, 2, 4, 6, or 8 in the ones place. A number that is a multiple of 2. Examples: 0, 4, and 678 are even numbers.

expanded form: A number written as the sum of the values of its digits. Example: 546 = 500 + 40 + 6.

expression: A combination of variables, numbers, and symbols that represent a mathematical relationship.

Glossary

face: The sides of a solid figure. For example, a cube has six faces that are all squares. The pyramid below has five faces—four triangles and one square.

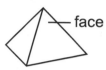

fact family: A group of related facts using the same numbers.
Example: 5 + 8 = 13; 13 – 8 = 5.

factor: One of two or more numbers that are multiplied together to give a product.
Example: In 4 x 3 = 12, 4 and 3 are factors of 12.

figure: A geometric figure is a set of points and/or lines in 2 or 3 dimensions.

flip (reflection): The change in a position of a figure that is the result of picking it up and turning it over.
Example: Reversing a "b" to a "d." Tipping a "p" to a "b" or a "b" to a "p" as shown below:

fraction: A symbol, such as $\frac{2}{8}$ or $\frac{5}{3}$, used to name a part of a whole, a part of a set, or a location on the number line.
Examples:

$$\frac{numerator}{denominator} = \frac{dividend}{divisor}$$

$$\frac{\text{\# of parts under consideration}}{\text{\# of parts in a set}}$$

function machine: Applies a function rule to a set of numbers, which determines a corresponding set of numbers.
Example: Input 9 ➞ Rule x 7 ➞ Output 63. If you apply the function rule "multiply by 7" to the values 5, 7, and 9, the corresponding values are:

$$5 \rightarrow 35$$
$$7 \rightarrow 49$$
$$9 \rightarrow 63$$

graph: A "picture" showing how certain facts are related to each other or how they compare to one another. Some examples of types of graphs are line graphs, pie charts, bar graphs, scatterplots, and pictographs.

grid: A pattern of regularly spaced horizontal and vertical lines on a plane that can be used to locate points and graph equations.

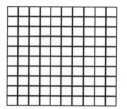

hexagon: A six-sided polygon. The total measure of the angles within a hexagon is 720°.

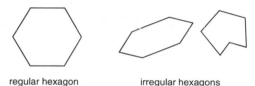

regular hexagon   irregular hexagons

impossible event: An event that can never happen.

integer: Any number, positive or negative, that is a whole number distance away from zero on a number line, in addition to zero. Specifically, an integer is any number in the set {. . .-3,-2,-1, 0, 1, 2, 3. . .}.
Examples of integers include: 1, 5, 273, -2, -35, and -1,375.

intersecting lines: Lines that cross at a point.
Examples:

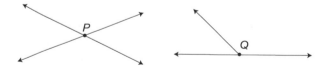

isosceles triangle: A triangle with at least two sides the same length.

justify: To prove or show to be true or valid using logic and/or evidence.

key: An explanation of what each symbol represents in a pictograph.

Glossary

kilometer (km): A metric unit of length: 1 kilometer = 1,000 meters.

line: A straight path of points that goes on forever in both directions.

line graph: A graph that uses a line or a curve to show how data changes over time.

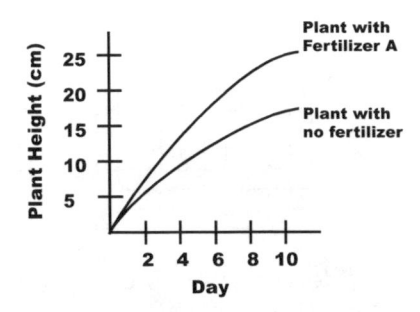

line of symmetry: A line on which a figure can be folded into two parts so that the parts match exactly.

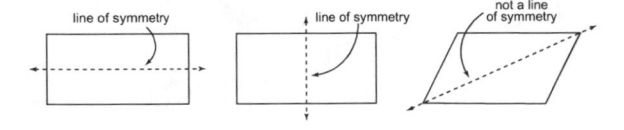

liter (L): A metric unit of capacity: 1 liter = 1,000 milliliters.

mass: The amount of matter an object has.

mean: Also called arithmetic average. A number found by adding two or more quantities together, and then dividing the sum by the number of quantities. For example, in the set {9, 5, 4} the mean is 6: 9 + 5 + 4 = 18; 18 ÷ 3 = 6. *See average.*

median: The middle number when numbers are put in order from least to greatest or from greatest to least. For example, in the set of numbers 6, 7, 8, 9, 10, the number 8 is the median (middle) number.

meter (m): A metric unit of length: 1 meter = 100 centimeters.

method: A systematic way of accomplishing a task.

mixed number: A number consisting of a whole number and a fraction. Example: $6\frac{2}{3}$.

mode: The number or numbers that occur most often in a set of data. Example: The mode of {1, 3, 4, 5, 5, 7, 9} is 5.

multiple: A product of a number and any other whole number. Examples: {2, 4, 6, 8, 10, 12,...} are multiples of 2.

multiplication: An operation on two numbers that tells how many in all. The first number is the number of sets and the second number tells how many in each set.

number line: A line that shows numbers in order using a scale. Equal intervals are marked and usually labeled on the number line.

number sentence: An expression of a relationship between quantities as an equation or an inequality. Examples: 7 + 7 = 8 + 6; 14 < 92; 56 + 4 > 59.

numerator: The top number in a fraction.

octagon: An eight-sided polygon. The total measure of the angles within an octagon is 1080°.

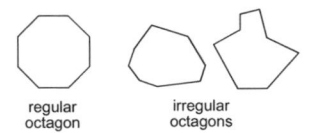

regular octagon   irregular octagons

odd number: A whole number that has 1, 3, 5, 7, or 9 in the ones place. An odd number is not divisible by 2. Examples: The numbers 53 and 701 are odd numbers.

operation: A mathematical process that combines numbers; basic operations of arithmetic include addition, subtraction, multiplication, and division.

order: To arrange numbers from the least to greatest or from the greatest to least.

ordered pair: Two numbers inside a set of parentheses separated by a comma that are used to name a point on a coordinate grid.

parallel lines: Lines in the same plane that never intersect.

parallelogram: A quadrilateral in which opposite sides are parallel.

pattern: An arrangement of numbers, pictures, etc., in an organized and predictable way. Examples: 3, 6, 9, 12, or ®0®0®0.

Glossary

pentagon: A five-sided polygon. The total measure of the angles within a pentagon is 540°.

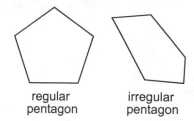

regular pentagon   irregular pentagon

perimeter: The distance around a figure.

perpendicular lines: Two lines that intersect to form a right angle (90 degrees).

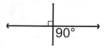

90°

pictograph: A graph that uses pictures or symbols to represent similar data. The value of each picture is interpreted by a "key" or "legend."

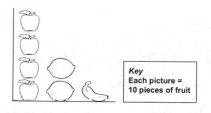

Key
Each picture =
10 pieces of fruit

place value: The value given to the place a digit has in a number.
Example: In the number 135, the 1 is in the hundreds place so it represents 100 (1 x 100); the 3 is in the tens place so it represents 30 (3 x 10); and the 5 is in the ones place so it represents 5 (5 x 1).

p.m.: The hours from noon to midnight; from the Latin words *post meridiem* meaning "after noon."

point: An exact position often marked by a dot.

polygon: A closed figure made up of straight line segments.

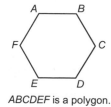

ABCDEF is a polygon.

possible event: An event that might or might not happen.

predict: To tell what you believe may happen in the future.

prediction: A prediction is a description of what may happen before it happens.

probability: The likelihood that something will happen.

product: The answer to a multiplication problem. Example: In 3 x 4 = 12, 12 is the product.

pyramid: A solid figure in which the base is a polygon and faces are triangles with a common point called a vertex.

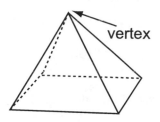

vertex

quadrilateral: A four-sided polygon. Rectangles, squares, parallelograms, rhombi, and trapezoids are all quadrilaterals. The total measure of the angles within a quadrilateral is 360°.
Example: *ABCD* is a quadrilateral.

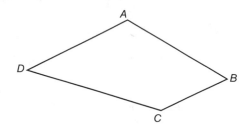

questionnaire: A set of questions for a survey.

quotient: The answer in a division problem.
Dividend ÷ divisor = quotient.
Example: In 15 ÷ 3 = 5, 5 is the quotient.

range: The difference between the least number and the greatest number in a data set. For example, in the set {4, 7, 10, 12, 36, 7, 2}, the range is 34; the greatest number (36) minus the least number (2): (36 – 2 = 34).

Glossary

rectangle: A quadrilateral with four right angles. A square is one example of a rectangle.

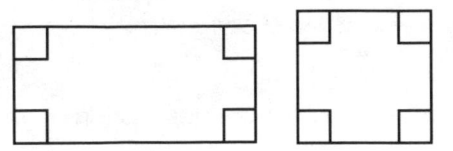

reflection: The change in the position of a figure that is the result of picking it up and turning it over. *See flip.*

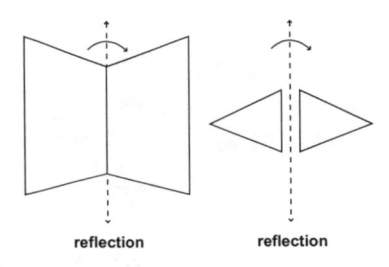

remainder: The number that is left over after dividing. Example: In 31 ÷ 7 = 4 R 3, the 3 is the remainder.

represent: To present clearly; describe; show.

rhombus: A quadrilateral with opposite sides parallel and all sides the same length. A square is one kind of rhombus.

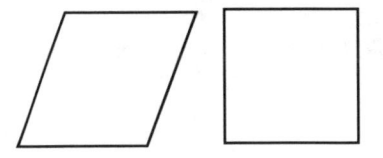

right angle: An angle that forms a square corner and measures 90 degrees.

right triangle: A triangle having one right angle. *See right angle and triangle.*

rounding: Replacing an exact number with a number that tells about how much or how many to the nearest ten, hundred, thousand, and so on.
Example: 52 rounded to the nearest 10 is 50.

rule: A procedure; a prescribed method; a way of describing the relationship between two sets of numbers. Example: In the following data, the rule is to add 3:

Input	Output
3	6
5	8
9	12

ruler: A straight-edged instrument used for measuring the lengths of objects. A ruler usually measures smaller units of length, such as inches or centimeters.

scale: The numbers that show the size of the units used on a graph.

sequence: A set of numbers arranged in a special order or pattern.

set: A group made up of numbers, figures, or parts.

side: A line segment connected to other segments to form the boundary of a polygon.

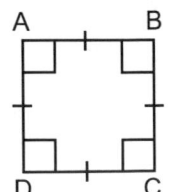

similar: A description for figures that have the same shape.

slide (translation): The change in the position of a figure that moves up, down, or sideways.
Example: scooting a book on a table.

solids: Figures in three dimensions.

solve: To find the solution to an equation or problem; finding the values of unknown variables that will make a true mathematical statement.

sphere: A solid figure in the shape of a ball. Example: A basketball is a sphere.

square: A rectangle with congruent (equal) sides. *See rectangle.*

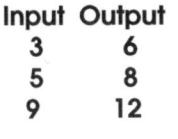

square number: The product of a number multiplied by itself.
Example: 49 is a square number (7 x 7 = 49).

square unit: A square with sides 1 unit long, used to measure area.

Glossary

standard form: A way to write a number showing only its digits. Example: 2,389.

standard units of measure: Units of measure commonly used; generally classified in the U.S. as the customary system or the metric system:

> **Customary System:**
> **Length**
> 1 foot (ft) = 12 inches (in)
> 1 yard (yd) = 3 feet or 36 inches
> 1 mile (mi) = 1,760 yards or 5,280 feet
>
> **Weight**
> 16 ounces (oz) = 1 pound (lb)
> 2,000 pounds = 1 ton (t)
>
> **Capacity**
> 1 pint (pt) = 2 cups (c)
> 1 quart (qt) = 2 pints
> 1 gallon (gal) = 4 quarts

> **Metric System:**
> **Length**
> 1 centimeter (cm) = 10 millimeters (mm)
> 1 decimeter (dm) = 10 centimeters
> 1 meter (m) = 100 centimeters
> 1 kilometer (km) = 1,000 meters
>
> **Weight**
> 1,000 milligrams (mg) = 1 gram (g)
> 1,000 grams (g) = 1 kilogram (kg)
> 1,000 kilograms (kg) = 1 tonne (metric ton)
>
> **Capacity**
> 1 liter (l) = 1,000 milliliters (ml)

strategy: A plan used in problem solving, such as looking for a pattern, drawing a diagram, working backward, etc.

subtraction: The operation that finds the difference between two numbers.

sum: The answer when adding two or more addends. Addend + Addend = Sum.

summary: A series of statements containing evidence, facts, and/or procedures that support a result.

survey: A way to collect data by asking a certain number of people the same question and recording their answers.

symmetry: A figure has line symmetry if it can be folded along a line so that both parts match exactly. A figure has radial or rotational symmetry if, after a rotation of less than 360°, it is indistinguishable from its former image.

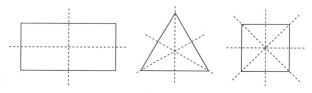
Examples of Figures With At Least Two Lines of Symmetry

table: A method of displaying data in rows and columns.

temperature: A measure of hot or cold in degrees.

translation (slide): A change in the position of a figure that moves it up, down, or sideways.

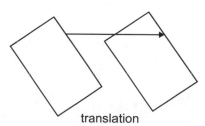
translation

triangle: A polygon with three sides. The sum of the angles of a triangle is always equal to 180°.

turn: The change in the position of a figure that moves it around a point. Also called a rotation.
Example: The hands of a clock turn around the center of the clock in a clockwise direction.

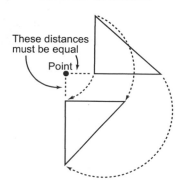
These distances must be equal
Point

Glossary

unlikely event: An event that probably will not happen.

vertex: The point where two rays meet to form an angle or where the sides of a polygon meet, or the point where 3 or more edges meet in a solid figure.

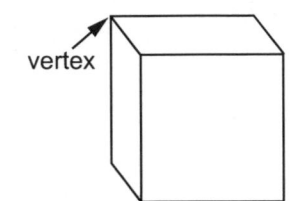

whole number: An integer in the set {0, 1, 2, 3 . . .}. In other words, a whole number is any number used when counting in addition to zero.

word forms: The number written in words. Examples: 546 is "five hundred forty-six."

Examples of Common Two-Dimensional Geometric Shapes

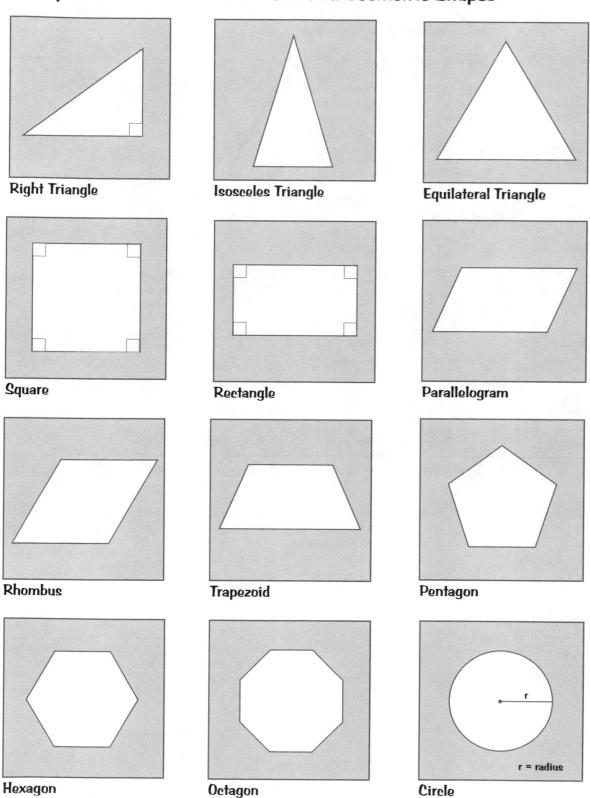

Right Triangle   **Isosceles Triangle**   **Equilateral Triangle**

Square   **Rectangle**   **Parallelogram**

Rhombus   **Trapezoid**   **Pentagon**

Hexagon   **Octagon**   **Circle**

r = radius

Examples of How Lines Interact

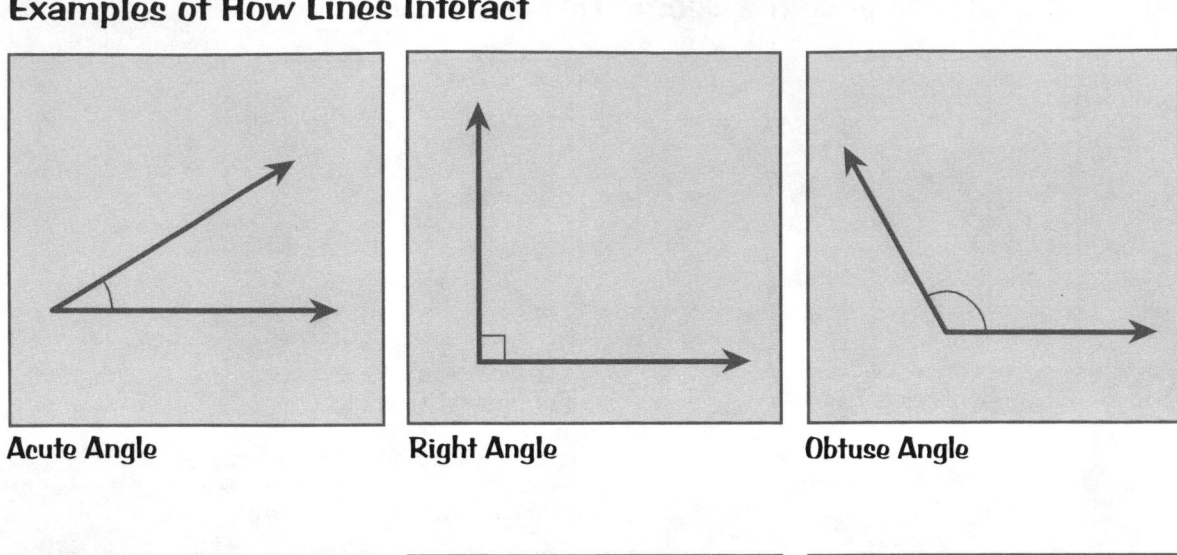

Acute Angle   **Right Angle**   **Obtuse Angle**

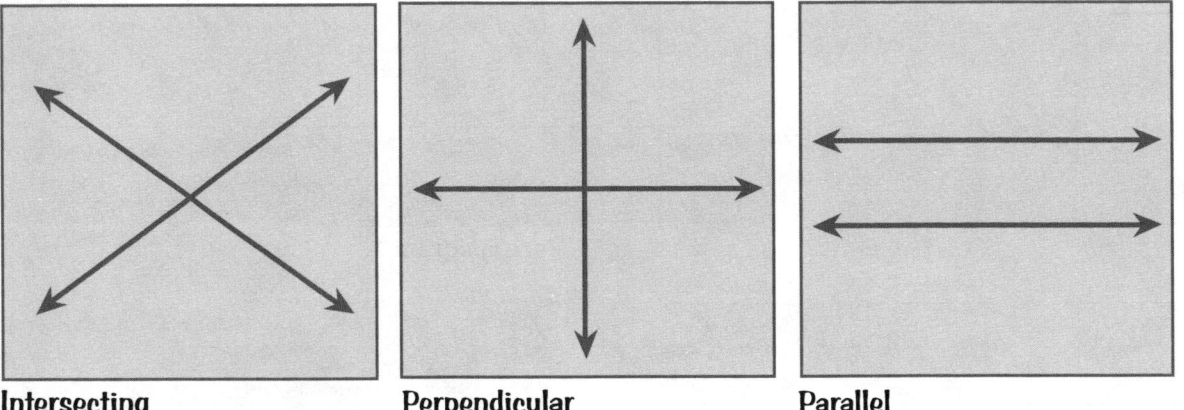

Intersecting   **Perpendicular**   **Parallel**

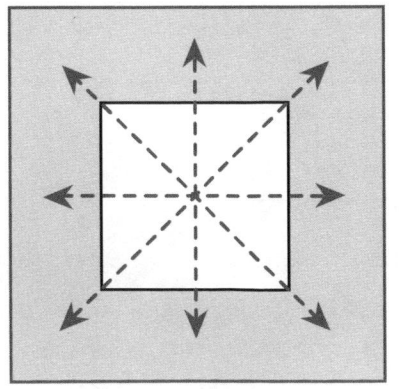

Lines of Symmetry

Examples of Common Types of Graphs

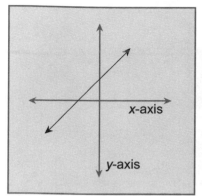

Line Graph

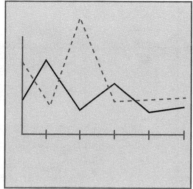

Double Line Graph

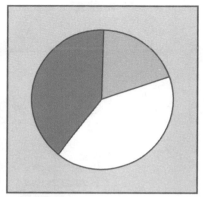

Pie Chart

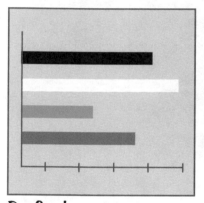

Bar Graph

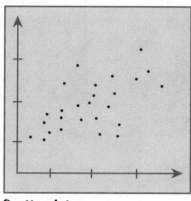

Scatterplot

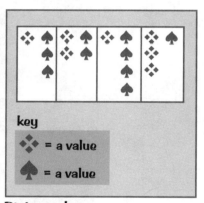

Pictograph

Examples of Common Three-Dimensional Objects

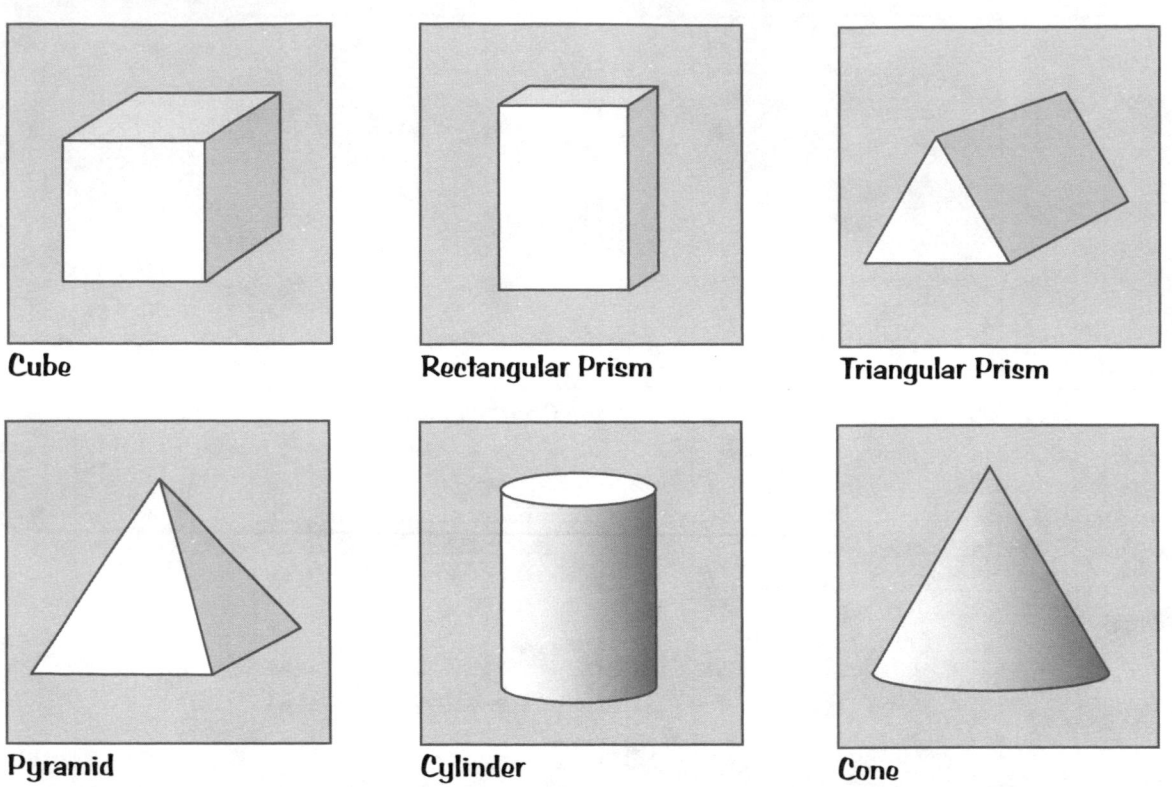

Cube   **Rectangular Prism**   **Triangular Prism**

Pyramid   **Cylinder**   **Cone**

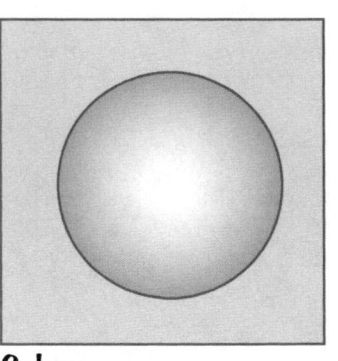

Sphere

Examples of Object Movement

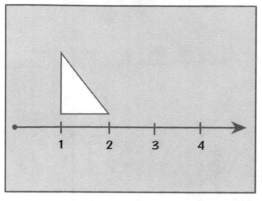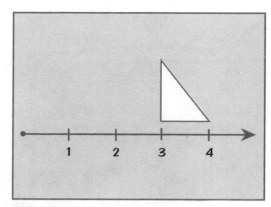

Translation

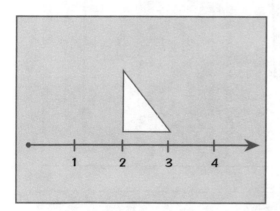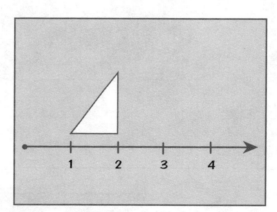

Reflection

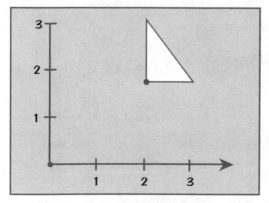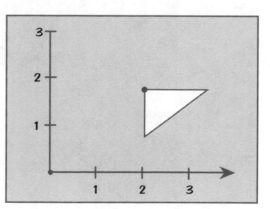

Rotation

Mathematics Assessment One

Responses *Throughout this section, pages from Mathematics Assessment One of the Student Workbook are included in reduced-page format. Correct multiple-choice answers and sample responses for each constructed-response item are indicated.*

Directions:

This Grade 7 Mathematics Assessment has multiple-choice and short-answer questions.

There are several important things to remember as you take this test:

- Read each multiple-choice question carefully. Think about what is being asked. Then fill in one answer bubble to mark your answer.

- If you do not know the answer to a multiple-choice question, skip it and go on. If you have time, go back to the questions you skipped and answer them.

- For short-answer questions, write your response clearly and neatly in the box provided.

- If you finish the Assessment early, go back and check over your work.

Mathematics Assessment One

$3 \times 3 = 9$
$\times 7$

Directions for Taking the Mathematics Assessment

The Mathematics Assessment is made up of multiple-choice and short-answer questions. These questions show you how the skills you have learned in Mathematics class may be tested. The questions also give you a chance to practice your skills. If you have trouble with an area, talk with a parent or teacher.

Multiple-choice questions require you to pick the best answer out of four possible choices. Only one answer is correct. The short-answer questions will ask you to write your answer and explain your thinking using words, numbers, or pictures, or to show the steps you used to solve a problem. Remember to read the questions and the answer choices carefully. You will mark your answers on the answer document.

When you finish, check your answers.

1. Ellie read $4\frac{1}{2}$ pages in $\frac{1}{4}$ hour.

At this rate, how many pages can she read per hour?

A. $\frac{1}{2}$ page per minute

B. 9 pages per hour

C. 10 pages per hour

✗ D. 18 pages per hour

2. Wayne's total body weight (*b*) equals 113 pounds. His body weight is roughly 14 times the weight of his head (*h*).

Which equation represents the proportional relationship between Wayne's body weight and the weight of his head?

✗ A. $b = 14h$

B. $b = 113$

C. $b = 14(b - h)$

D. $b = h + 113$

3. Look at the graph.

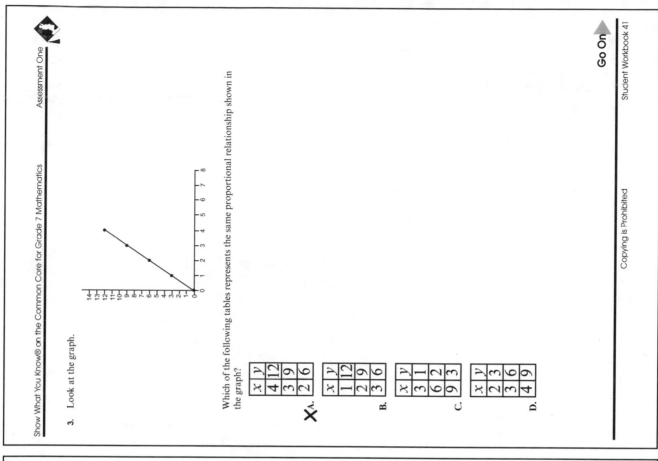

Which of the following tables represents the same proportional relationship shown in the graph?

✗ A.

x	y
4	12
3	9
2	6

B.

x	y
1	12
2	9
3	6

C.

x	y
3	1
6	2
9	3

D.

x	y
2	3
3	6
4	9

Assessment One   Show What You Know® on the Common Core for Grade 7 Mathematics

4. Ivy and her family celebrated her birthday at her favorite Mexican restaurant. The bill came to $39.00. Since the food and service were excellent, Ivy's dad wanted to leave a 20% tip.

How much did he leave?

A. $3.90
✗ B. $7.80
C. $9.75
D. $11.70

5. A $15.00 music CD is selling for $10.50.

How much of a discount off the regular price is this?

A. 10.5%
B. 20%
✗ C. 30%
D. 45%

6. Which of the following situations has -16 as the result?

A. 16 - 20
B. 16 - 0
C. 40 - 24
✗ D. 24 - 40

7. Look at the expression.

$$-5 \times -5 \ \boxed{} \ -(5 \times 5)$$

Which of the following symbols would create a true mathematical statement when placed between the two expressions?

A. =
B. <
C. ≤
✗ D. >

Show What You Know® on the Common Core for Grade 7 Mathematics   Assessment One

8. Which fraction results in the decimal 0.444....?

A. $\frac{1}{4}$
B. $\frac{444}{1,000}$
✗ C. $\frac{4}{9}$
D. $\frac{4}{4}$

9. Which of the following operations would provide an answer greater than 1?

A. multiplying two positive fractions that are each less than 1
B. multiplying two negative fractions that are each greater than -1
✗ C. multiplying two negative fractions that are each less than -1
D. multiplying a negative fraction that is less than -1 and a positive fraction that is greater than 1

10. After a school fundraiser, the treasurer, Stan, tallies the income for a total of one hundred twenty-five dollars. Stan subtracts one hundred thirty-five dollars in expenses from the income for a loss of ten dollars.

Which integer represents the difference between income and expenses?

A. 10
✗ B. -10
C. 125
D. 135

11. Look at the expression.

$$2(3r + 1) - (r + 1)$$

Simplify the expression.

A. 5r
✗ B. 5r + 1
C. 5r + 3
D. 7r + 1

16. The perimeter of a rectangular yard is 420 feet. The length of the yard is 120 feet.

What is the width of the yard?

Using the perimeter equation gives you $2w + (2 \cdot 120) = 420$. Simplify this equation.

$2w + 240 = 420$

$2w = 180$

$w = 90$

17. The sketch below is a scale drawing of a room.

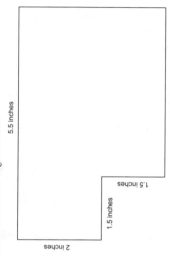

Scale: 1 inch = 1.5 yards

(dimensions shown: 5.5 inches, 2 inches, 1.5 inches, 1.5 inches, 4 inches)

What is the length, in yards, of the unlabeled wall?

A. 3.5 yards

B. 5 yards

✗ C. 5.25 yards

D. 7.5 yards

Go On

---

12. A secretary purchased three items at an office supply store. Including a 6.5% sales tax, her total payment was $13.85.

Which equation can be used to correctly determine the cost of the three items before tax?

A. $6.5x = 13.85$

✗ B. $.065x + x = 13.85$

C. $13.85 - x = 6.5$

D. $13.85 = .065x$

13. Louisa works as a clown in a circus. When she started working, she earned $12,000 the first year. For each year after the first, she was told she would receive a raise of 5% of her yearly salary each year.

If this is the third year Louisa has worked in the circus, what is her yearly salary for this year?

A. $12,600

B. $13,200

✗ C. $13,230

D. $13,800

14. Rahkeem bought $4\frac{3}{4}$ yards of fabric at $2.80 per yard and $2\frac{1}{2}$ yards of ribbon at $1.80 per yard. He paid a sales tax of 5%.

Calculate Rahkeem's total cost including tax.

Rahkeem's total bill is $18.69. This problem involves both fractional and decimal numbers. It is often easiest to convert the fractional numbers to decimals before the calculations. In this case, 4 3/4 x $2.80 can be expressed as 4.75 x $2.80, which equals $13.30. Also, 2 1/2 x $1.80 can be expressed as 2.5 x $1.80, which equals $4.50. These two products add together for equal $17.80 ($13.30 + $4.50 = $17.80). This is the total before tax. To find the tax, we multiply the total by the decimal equivalent of 5% ($17.80 x 0.05 = $0.89). The tax is $0.89. To get the final cost, add the total cost of the fabric and the ribbon to the tax; $17.80 + $0.89 = $18.69.

15. At a local mall, the owners have decided to redesign the parking lot. When the parking lot is completed, there will be 5 fewer than 3 times the original number of parking spaces in the lot.

If there will be 448 parking spaces in the parking lot when it is completed, which of the following equations could be used to find the number of parking spaces (n) currently in the parking lot?

A. $448 = (3 \times 5) - n$

✗ B. $448 = (3 \times n) - 5$

C. $448 = 3 \times (5 - n)$

D. $448 = 3 \times (n - 5)$

Go On

18. For homework, Brad was asked to draw several triangles.

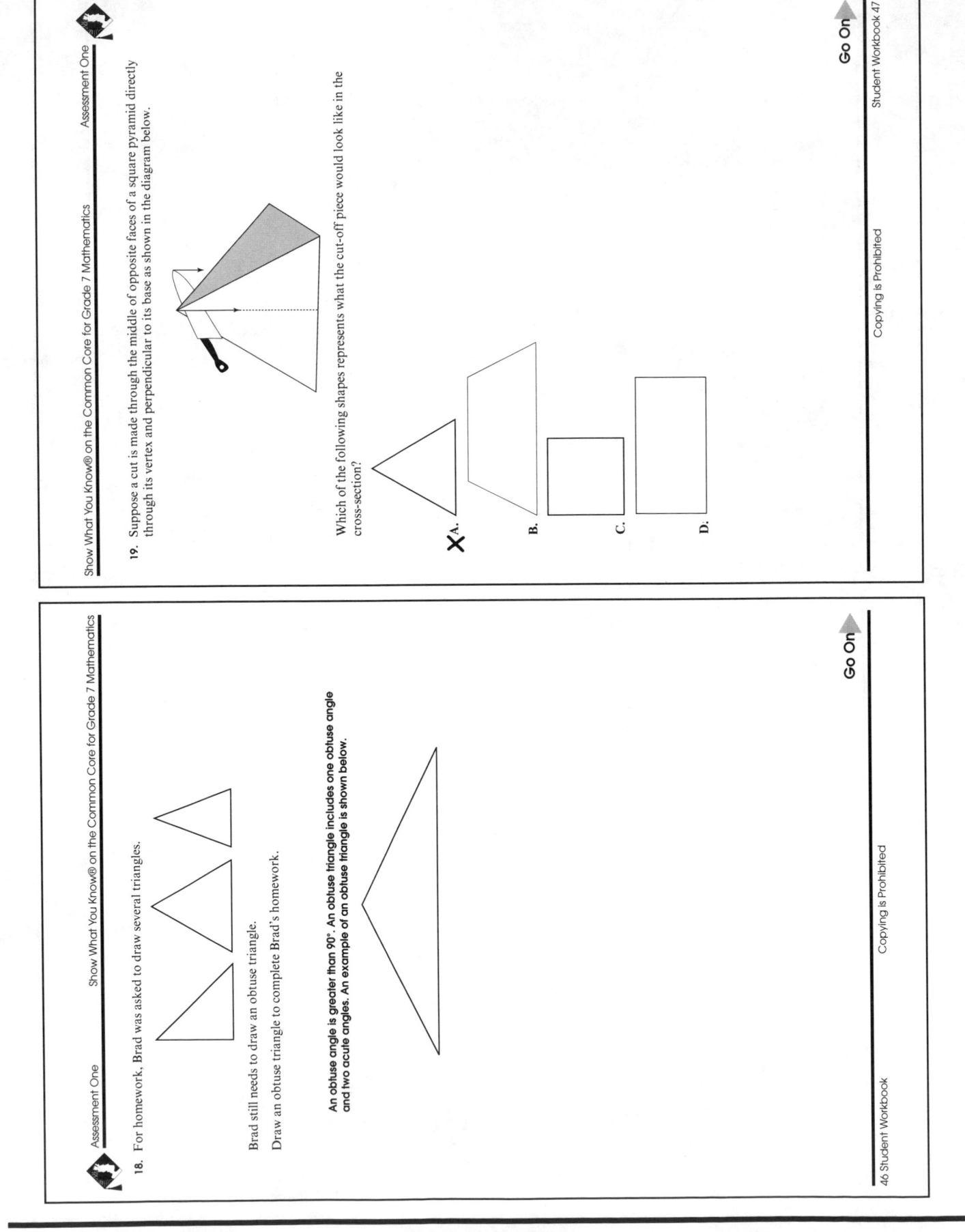

Brad still needs to draw an obtuse triangle.

Draw an obtuse triangle to complete Brad's homework.

An obtuse angle is greater than 90°. An obtuse triangle includes one obtuse angle and two acute angles. An example of an obtuse triangle is shown below.

---

19. Suppose a cut is made through the middle of opposite faces of a square pyramid directly through its vertex and perpendicular to its base as shown in the diagram below.

Which of the following shapes represents what the cut-off piece would look like in the cross-section?

X A.

B.

C.

D.

---

23. Use the protractor below to find the measure of each angle.

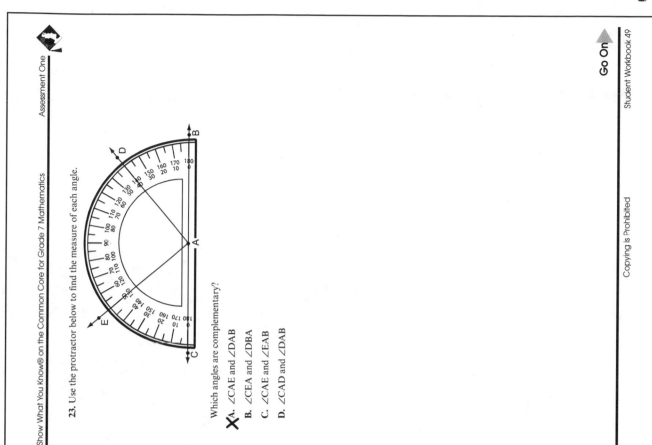

Which angles are complementary?

✗A. ∠CAE and ∠DAB

B. ∠CEA and ∠DBA

C. ∠CAE and ∠EAB

D. ∠CAD and ∠DAB

Go On

---

20. The Union Pacific Big Boy was the largest steam locomotive ever built. The locomotive had 24 wheels, 16 of which were 68-inch drive wheels.

If a drive wheel from this locomotive is 68 inches in diameter, what is its circumference? ($C = 2\pi r$ or $C = \pi d$.)

A. approximately 68 inches or about $5\frac{1}{2}$ feet

B. approximately 107 inches or about 9 feet

✗C. approximately 214 inches or about 18 feet

D. approximately 427 inches or about $35\frac{1}{2}$ feet

21. Thomasina needs to determine the area of a circle with a diameter of 30 feet.

What is the area of this circle?

Using the formula $A = \pi r^2$ and realizing if the diameter is 30, the radius must be 15 (3.14 • 15 • 15 = 706.5).

22. The formula for the circumference of a circle is $C = 2\pi(r)$.

Using 3.1415 as a value for π, what would be the radius of a circle with a circumference of 125.66 cm?

A. 10

B. 12

C. 18

✗D. 20

Go On

24. Study the drawing below. A wedding cake is made up of three layers, and each layer is a rectangular prism smaller than the layer beneath it.

What is the total volume of the wedding cake? All measurements are in inches.

A. 174 inches³

B. 363 inches³

C. 510 inches³

X D. 537 inches³

Go On

---

25. Which of the following is a characteristic of a useful sample?

X A. It is representative of the population you are studying.

B. It has enough diversity so the results don't void the study.

C. It is at least 1% of the overall population being studied.

D. It is at least 4% of the overall population being studied.

26. A random sampling of 125 people were asked what size of shoes they wear. Sixty percent of the people surveyed said they wear size 10 shoes.

In a population of 2,000 people, about how many people would wear the size 10 shoes?

A. 960 people

B. 1,000 people

X C. 1,200 people

D. 1,360 people

27. Ray and Larry are sampling the fish population of a pond. They want to know about how many fish are in the pond. In the first sample of 100 fish, they place tags on all the fish and release them back into the pond. In the next sample of 100 fish, 19 of the fish have tags on them.

Using this information, what is the approximate population of fish in the pond?

A. 123 fish

X B. 526 fish

C. 1,900 fish

D. 1,919 fish

Go On

---

29. The spinner below is used in a board game.

Which of the following statements about this spinner is **not** true?

　A. Spinning the color blue is most likely.

✗B. Spinning red or spinning green are equally likely.

　C. Spinning the color green is least likely.

　D. Spinning red or spinning yellow are equally likely.

30. Each side of a 6-sided die is painted one of three colors. Three of the sides are painted black, 2 of the sides are painted blue, and the remaining side is painted red.

When the die is rolled 60 times, which of these events is closest to its expected probability as predicted by mathematics?

　A. A black side is rolled 40 times.

✗B. A blue side is rolled 20 times.

　C. The red side is rolled 15 times.

　D. A black side is rolled 15 times.

---

28. The table below shows the frequency of scores in two of Mr. Mathly's classes on the most recent quiz.

Test Score	Class A Frequency	Class B Frequency
3	1	6
4	2	0
5	3	0
6	4	2
7	3	2
8	0	5
9	2	0
10	0	2

Which choice correctly compares the medians of both classes?

　A. The medians are the same for both classes.

✗B. Class A's median is 1 point lower than class B's.

　C. Class A's median is 3 points lower than class B's.

　D. Class B's median is 2 points higher than class A's.

31. Mark rolls a 6-sided die seven times. He has rolled a 6 twice, a 5 twice, and a 2 three times.

What is the probability that he will roll another 2?

A. $\frac{3}{7}$

✗ B. $\frac{1}{6}$

C. $\frac{2}{7}$

D. $\frac{1}{3}$

32. Phyllis has a box of cookies. There are 6 sugar cookies in the box, and there are 8 oatmeal cookies in the box. If Phyllis takes a cookie from the box without looking, what is the probability she will get an oatmeal cookie?

A. $\frac{3}{7}$

✗ B. $\frac{4}{7}$

C. $\frac{3}{4}$

D. $\frac{4}{3}$

33. To select the Student of the Week, Mr. Jones puts all of his students' names in a hat. When a student is selected, his or her name is not put back into the hat. There are 13 boys and 13 girls in the class. The first three weeks of school, three boys were chosen as Student of the Week.

For the fourth week, what is the probability that a girl's name will be selected?

A. $\frac{13}{26}$

B. $\frac{10}{23}$

✗ C. $\frac{13}{23}$

D. $\frac{10}{26}$

34. Marcy invented a game where first she would spin Spinner A and then spin Spinner B.

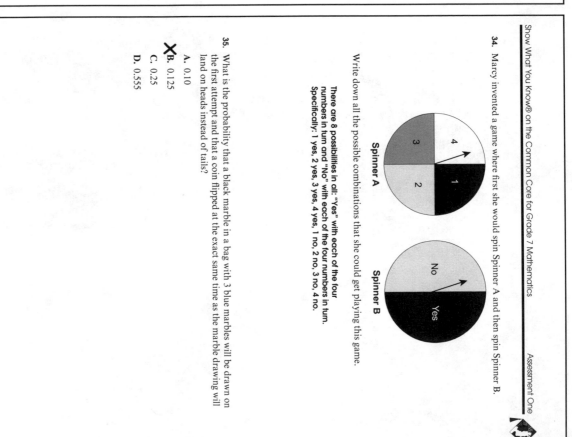

Spinner A   Spinner B

Write down all the possible combinations that she could get playing this game.

There are 8 possibilities in all: "Yes" with each of the four numbers in turn and "No" with each of the four numbers in turn.
Specifically: 1 yes, 2 yes, 3 yes, 4 yes, 1 no, 2 no, 3 no, 4 no.

35. What is the probability that a black marble in a bag with 3 blue marbles will be drawn on the first attempt and that a coin flipped at the exact same time as the marble drawing will land on heads instead of tails?

A. 0.10

✗ B. 0.125

C. 0.25

D. 0.555

36. Carissa's mathematics teacher drew intersecting lines on the board.

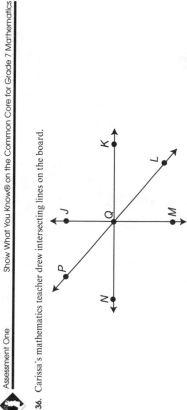

Which phrase best describes $\angle NQP$ and $\angle LQK$ as a pair of angles?

A. adjacent angles

B. complementary angles

C. supplementary angles

X D. vertical angles

37. After taking a keyboarding class, Raul is able to type 35 words per minute.

At this rate, how long will it take him to type a 7,000-word term paper?

X A. 200 minutes

B. 60 minutes

C. 20 minutes

D. 0.0005 hour

Go On

---

38. At a school raffle, students and parents put their name into a box for a drawing. Twenty-four adults and 52 students put their names in the box.

What is the probability of drawing out the name of an adult?

A. $\frac{1}{24}$

B. $\frac{24}{52}$

X C. $\frac{24}{76}$

D. $\frac{52}{24}$

39. The table below is a sample space of all possible number combinations from two standard dice.

Second Die

		1	2	3	4	5	6
First Die	1	1+1=2	1+2=3	1+3=4	1+4=5	1+5=6	1+6=7
	2	2+1=3	2+2=4	2+3=5	2+4=6	2+5=7	2+6=8
	3	3+1=4	3+2=5	3+3=6	3+4=7	3+5=8	3+6=9
	4	4+1=5	4+2=6	4+3=7	4+4=8	4+5=9	4+6=10
	5	5+1=6	5+2=7	5+3=8	5+4=9	5+5=10	5+6=11
	6	6+1=7	6+2=8	6+3=9	6+4=10	6+5=11	6+6=12

What is the probability of rolling a 3 or a 9 on one roll of two fair dice?

X A. $\frac{1}{6}$

B. $\frac{1}{9}$

C. $\frac{1}{12}$

D. $\frac{1}{18}$

Go On

40. Look at the shapes below.

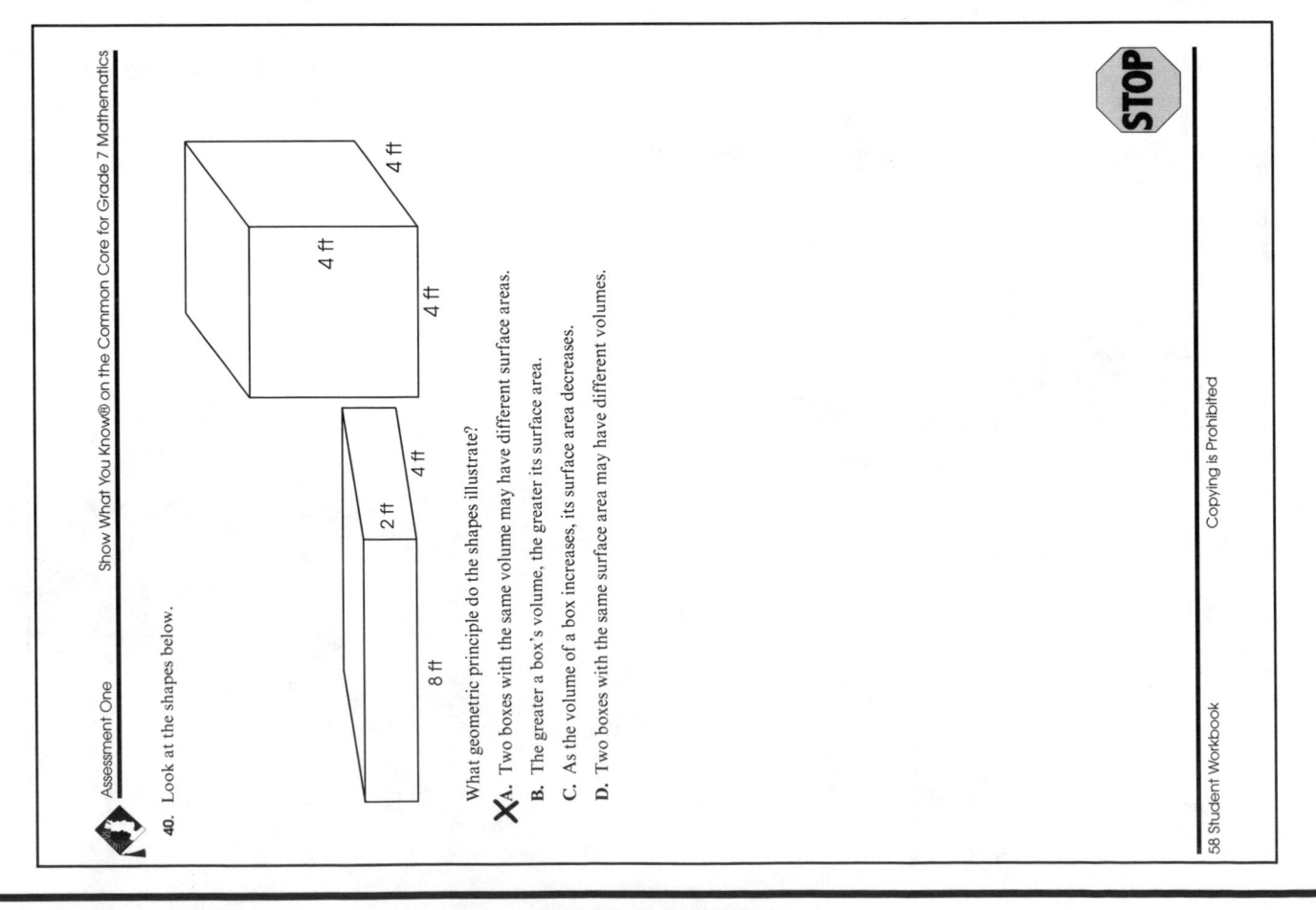

What geometric principle do the shapes illustrate?

A. Two boxes with the same volume may have different surface areas.

B. The greater a box's volume, the greater its surface area.

C. As the volume of a box increases, its surface area decreases.

D. Two boxes with the same surface area may have different volumes.

---

1. Ⓐ Ⓑ Ⓒ ●
2. ● Ⓑ Ⓒ Ⓓ
3. ● Ⓑ Ⓒ Ⓓ
4. Ⓐ ● Ⓒ Ⓓ
5. Ⓐ Ⓑ ● Ⓓ
6. Ⓐ Ⓑ Ⓒ ●
7. Ⓐ Ⓑ Ⓒ ●
8. Ⓐ Ⓑ ● Ⓓ
9. Ⓐ Ⓑ ● Ⓓ
10. Ⓐ ● Ⓒ Ⓓ
11. Ⓐ ● Ⓒ Ⓓ
12. Ⓐ ● Ⓒ Ⓓ
13. Ⓐ Ⓑ ● Ⓓ

14.

> Rahkeem's total bill is $18.69. This problem involves both fractional and decimal numbers. It is often easiest to convert the fractional numbers to decimals before the calculations. In this case, 4 3/4 x $2.80 can be expressed as 4.75 x $2.80, which equals $13.30. Also, 2 1/2 x $1.80 can be expressed as 2.5 x $1.80, which equals $4.50. These two products add together to equal $17.80 ($13.30 + $4.50 = $17.80). This is the total before tax. To find the tax, we multiply the total by the decimal equivalent of 5% ($17.80 x 0.05 = $0.89). The tax is $0.89. To get the final cost, add the total cost of the fabric and the ribbon to the tax; $17.80 + $0.89 = $18.69.
>
> Rahkeem's total cost is _____ $18.69 _____ .

15 Ⓐ ● Ⓒ Ⓓ

16

Using the perimeter equation gives you $2w + (2 \cdot 120) = 420$.
Simplify this equation.
$2w + 240 = 420$
$2w = 180$
$w = 90$ feet

The width of the yard is _____90 feet_____ .

17 Ⓐ Ⓑ ● Ⓓ

18

An obtuse angle is greater than 90°. An obtuse triangle includes one obtuse angle and two acute angles. An example of an obtuse triangle is shown below.

19 ● Ⓑ Ⓒ Ⓓ

20 Ⓐ Ⓑ ● Ⓓ

21

Using the formula A = πr² and realizing if the diameter is 30, the radius must be 15 (3.14 • 15 • 15 = 706.5).

The area of the circle is _____15 feet_____ .

22 Ⓐ Ⓑ Ⓒ ●

23 ● Ⓑ Ⓒ Ⓓ

24 Ⓐ Ⓑ Ⓒ ●

25 ● Ⓑ Ⓒ Ⓓ

26 Ⓐ Ⓑ ● Ⓓ

27 Ⓐ ● Ⓒ Ⓓ

28 Ⓐ ● Ⓒ Ⓓ

29 Ⓐ ● Ⓒ Ⓓ

30 Ⓐ ● Ⓒ Ⓓ

31 Ⓐ ● Ⓒ Ⓓ

32 Ⓐ ● Ⓒ Ⓓ

33 Ⓐ Ⓑ ● Ⓓ

34

There are 8 possibilities in all: "Yes" with each of the four numbers in turn and "No" with each of the four numbers in turn. Specifically: 1 yes, 2 yes, 3 yes, 4 yes, 1 no, 2 no, 3 no, 4 no.

35 (A) ● (C) (D)

36 (A) (B) (C) ●

37 ● (B) (C) (D)

38 (A) (B) ● (D)

39 ● (B) (C) (D)

40 ● (B) (C) (D)

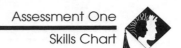

Question	Standard	Answer	Keywords
1	7.RP.1	D	Unit Rate, Fraction
2	7.RP.2	A	Proportion, Equation
3	7.RP.2	A	Proportion, Table
4	7.RP.3	B	Percent
5	7.RP.3	C	Percent
6	7.NS.1	D	Integers, Subtraction
7	7.NS.2	D	Integers, Multiplication
8	7.NS.2	C	Fraction, Decimal, Convert
9	7.NS.2	C	Rational Numbers, Multiplication, Integers, Fractions
10	7.NS.3	B	Integers, Subtraction
11	7.EE.1	B	Simplify, Algebraic Expression
12	7.EE.2	B	Percent, Equation
13	7.EE.3	C	Percent
14	7.EE.3	—	Percent, Sales Tax, Multi-Step
15	7.EE.4	B	Write Equation
16	7.EE.4	—	Solve Equations, Perimeter
17	7.G.1	C	Scale Drawing, Proportions
18	7.G.2	—	Geometric Figures, Draw, Triangle
19	7.G.3	A	Cross-Section, Three-Dimensional
20	7.G.4	C	Circumference, Circle

—see analysis for constructed response

Question	Standard	Answer	Keywords
21	7.G.4	—	Area, Circle
22	7.G.4	D	Circumference, Circle
23	7.G.5	A	Complementary, Angle Measurement
24	7.G.6	D	Volume, Rectangular Prism, Composite Figures
25	7.SP.1	A	Sample, Statistics
26	7.SP.2	C	Sampling, Prediction
27	7.SP.2	B	Sampling, Population Size
28	7.SP.4	B	Median, Compare Data
29	7.SP.5	B	Probability, Likelihood of Events
30	7.SP.6	B	Probability, Prediction
31	7.SP.7	B	Probability, Simple Event
32	7.SP.7	B	Probability, Simple Event
33	7.SP.7	C	Probability, Simple Event
34	7.SP.8	—	Sample Space, Outcomes
35	7.SP.8	B	Probability, Compound Events
36	7.G.5	D	Adjacent Angles, Angle Measurement
37	7.RP.3	A	Proportions
38	7.SP.7	C	Probability, Simple Event
39	7.SP.8	A	Probability, Compound Event
40	7.G.6	A	Volume, Surface Area, Rectangular Prism

—*see analysis for constructed response*

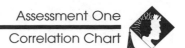

Mathematics Assessment One: Correlation Chart

Use this chart to identify areas for improvement for individual students or for the class as a whole. For example, enter students' names in the left-hand column. When a student misses a question, place an "X" in the corresponding box. A column with a large number of "Xs" shows that the class needs more practice with that particular objective.

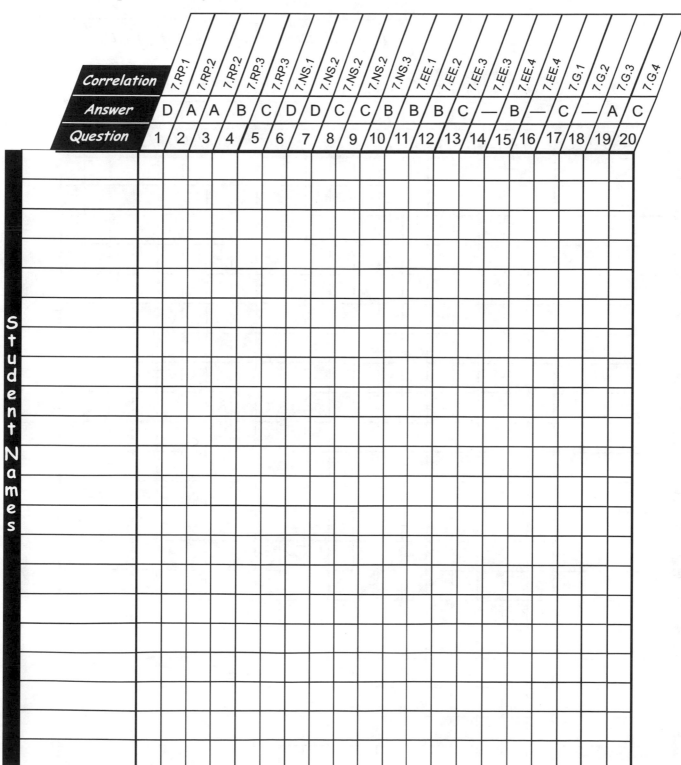

Correlation	7.RP.1	7.RP.2	7.RP.2	7.RP.3	7.RP.3	7.NS.1	7.NS.2	7.NS.2	7.NS.2	7.NS.3	7.EE.1	7.EE.2	7.EE.3	7.EE.3	7.EE.4	7.EE.4	7.G.1	7.G.2	7.G.3	7.G.4
Answer	D	A	A	B	C	D	D	C	C	B	B	B	C	—	B	—	C	—	A	C
Question	1	2	3	4	5	6	7	8	9	10	11	12	13	14	15	16	17	18	19	20

Student Names

—see analysis for constructed response

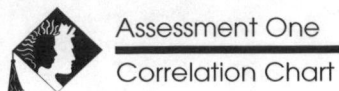

Correlation	7.G.4	7.G.4	7.G.5	7.G.6	7.SP.1	7.SP.2	7.SP.2	7.SP.4	7.SP.5	7.SP.6	7.SP.7	7.SP.7	7.SP.7	7.SP.8	7.SP.8	7.G.5	7.RP.3	7.SP.7	7.SP.8	7.G.6
Answer	—	D	A	D	A	C	B	B	B	B	B	B	C	—	B	D	A	C	A	A
Question	21	22	23	24	25	26	27	28	29	30	31	32	33	34	35	36	37	38	39	40

Student Names

—*see analysis for constructed response*

Mathematics Assessment Two

Responses *Throughout this section, pages from Mathematics Assessment Two of the Student Workbook are included in reduced-page format. Correct multiple-choice answers and sample responses for each constructed-response item are indicated.*

Mathematics Assessment Two

Directions for Taking the Mathematics Assessment

The Mathematics Assessment is made up of multiple-choice and short-answer questions. These questions show you how the skills you have learned in Mathematics class may be tested. The questions also give you a chance to practice your skills. If you have trouble with an area, talk with a parent or teacher.

Multiple-choice questions require you to pick the best answer out of four possible choices. Only one answer is correct. The short-answer questions will ask you to write your answer and explain your thinking using words, numbers, or pictures, or to show the steps you used to solve a problem. Remember to read the questions and the answer choices carefully. You will mark your answers on the answer document.

When you finish, check your answers.

Directions:

This Grade 7 Mathematics Assessment has multiple-choice and short-answer questions.

There are several important things to remember as you take this test:

- Read each multiple-choice question carefully. Think about what is being asked. Then fill in one answer bubble to mark your answer.

- If you do not know the answer to a multiple-choice question, skip it and go on. If you have time, go back to the questions you skipped and answer them.

- For short-answer questions, write your response clearly and neatly in the box provided.

- If you finish the Assessment early, go back and check over your work.

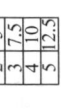

3. Which of the following equations represents the same proportion shown in this table?

x	y
2	5
3	7.5
4	10
5	12.5

A. $y = x + 3$

X B. $y = 2.5x$

C. $y = 2x + 1$

D. $y = 2x + 2$

4. A real estate agent will receive a 3% commission from the sale of a house that sold for $218,800.

How much money will the agent earn from this sale?

A. $6,024

X B. $6,564

C. $7,800

D. $12,200

Go On

1. Caden rode his bike $2\frac{1}{2}$ miles in $\frac{1}{2}$ hour. How many miles per hour did he ride?

A. $1\frac{1}{2}$ miles per hour

B. 4 miles per hour

X C. 5 miles per hour

D. 6 miles per hour

2. A direct variation is a proportional relationship with an equation in the form $y = kx$, where k is a fixed number other than zero. In problem situations involving direct variation, you can say, "y varies directly as x, or y is directly proportional to x."

Using this definition and what you know about proportions, which statement below is false?

A. The graphs of all direct variations are straight lines.

B. The graphs of all direct variations pass through the origin.

C. The values in this chart represent a direct variation:

x	3	4	5	6	7
y	6	8	10	12	14

X D. If y varies directly as x, and $y = 5$ when $x = 4$, then $x = 15$ when $y = 12$.

Go On

5. Andrew's parents told him that if he got an A in math for the first semester, they would buy him a new laptop computer that costs $750. When Andrew's parents went to buy the laptop, they found that the price had dropped to $600.

How much of a savings does this represent?

A. 80%

B. 25%

X C. 20%

D. 15%

6. Which of the following situations has -4 as the result?

A. 11 − 7

X B. 6 − 10

C. 4 − 0

D. 4 − 7

7. When any positive integer is divided by -2, which of the following statements will be true?

A. The answer will be greater than the original integer.

X B. The answer will be negative.

C. The answer will be even.

D. The answer will be odd.

8. Solve the following equation.

$$\frac{1}{4} \times 0.8 = \boxed{}$$

Show or explain your work using words, numbers, and/or pictures.

First convert the fraction 1/4 to a decimal, 0.25. Then multiply: 0.25 × 0.8 = 0.2.

---

9. Which operation would provide an answer greater than 0 and less than 1?

A. multiplying two positive fractions that are each greater than 1

X B. multiplying two negative fractions that are each greater than -1

C. multiplying two negative fractions that are each less than -1

D. multiplying 1 and a negative fraction that is less than -1

10. Which of these operations results in the lowest value?

A. -4 − (-20)

B. -4 ÷ (-20)

C. -4 × (-20)

X D. -4 + (-20)

11. Simplify the expression.

$$-4(2a - 3) + 5a$$

A. 3(a − 4)

X B. -3(a − 4)

C. -3(a + 4)

D. 3(a + 4)

12. Sarah and Ashley went to the mall to buy clothes. If dresses are marked 30% off, which of the following expressions could be used to calculate the sale price of a dress when p represents the price of the dress?

A. 0.30 × p

B. p − 0.30

C. (p − 0.30) × p

X D. p − 0.30 × p

13. What is the total price of 3 paperback books if the books cost $12.00 each and the sales tax is 6%.?

A. $12.72

B. $36.00

C. $36.06

✗ D. $38.16

14. Saleem is buying 3 notebooks for $1.60 each, 5 packs of pencils for $1.20 per pack, and a calculator for $16.80. The sales tax on these items is 5%.

Write an expression that can be used to calculate the sales tax on this purchase.

Evaluate the expression to find the total amount of the sales tax Saleem pays on this purchase.

0.05(3 × $1.60 + 5 × $1.20 + $16.80) **First find the cost of the notebooks by multiplying $1.60 by 3, then find the cost of the pencils by multiplying $1.20 by 5. Next add these two products to $16.80, the cost of the calculator and multiply this total by 0.05 the decimal equivalent of 5%.**

0.05(3 × $1.60 + 5 × $1.20 + $16.80) = 0.05($4.80 + $6.00 + $16.80) = 0.05($27.60) = $1.38 **Saleem pays $1.38 in sales tax.**

---

15. Ben likes to sell baseball cards from his collection online. He sets the price for a card at twice what he paid for it plus $5.00 for shipping.

If we let c represent the cost to the buyer and b represent the price Ben paid for a card, which of these equations shows how Ben prices his cards?

A. $c = 10b$

B. $b = 2c + 5$

✗ C. $c = 2b + 5$

D. $b = 5c + b$

16. A rectangular prism with a width of 20 inches and a length of 60 inches has a volume of 2,400 cubic inches.

Rectangular Prism

60 in

20 in

What is the height of this prism? (*Note: Prism in diagram not drawn to scale.*)

✗ A. 2 inches

B. 10 inches

C. 12 inches

D. 24 inches

17. The Taipei 101 Building in Taipei, Taiwan, is currently the world's second tallest building at 1,670 feet.

If you are making a scale model of this building where 1 inch equals 20 feet, about how tall must your model be? Express your answer to the nearest whole foot.

X **A.** 7 feet

B. 20 feet

C. 84 feet

D. 139 feet

18. Draw a figure that has two acute angles and two obtuse angles.

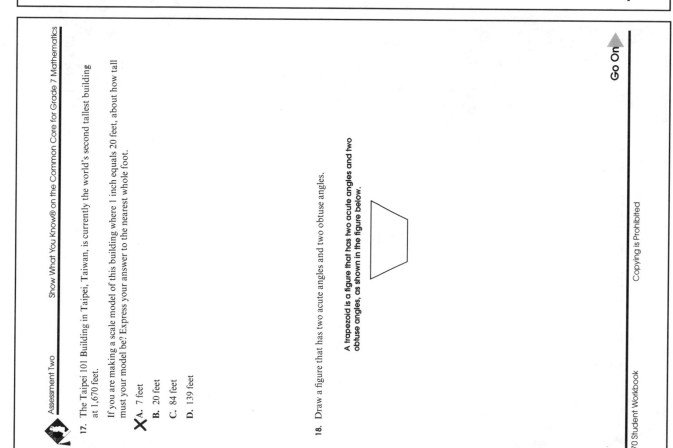

A trapezoid is a figure that has two acute angles and two obtuse angles, as shown in the figure below.

---

19. Suppose a cut is made through a square pyramid perpendicular to its base as shown in the diagram below.

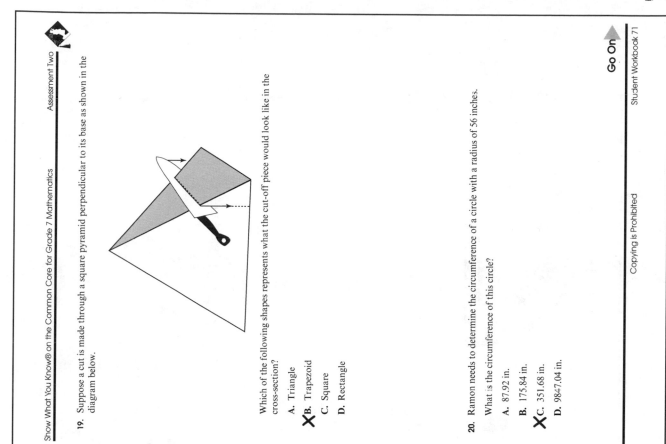

Which of the following shapes represents what the cut-off piece would look like in the cross-section?

A. Triangle

X **B.** Trapezoid

C. Square

D. Rectangle

20. Ramon needs to determine the circumference of a circle with a radius of 56 inches.

What is the circumference of this circle?

A. 87.92 in.

B. 175.84 in.

X **C.** 351.68 in.

D. 9847.04 in.

21. Which of the following is the **best** estimate for the area of a circle with a radius of 11 inches?

   A. 200 square inches

   B. 300 square inches

✗ C. 400 square inches

   D. 450 square inches

22. If a circle has a circumference of 44, what is the value of its diameter?

Show or explain your work using words, numbers, and/or pictures.

In this case, when solving, it is easier to use the fraction form of π.

So, 44 = d(22/7); 308 = 22d; d = 14.

---

23. Use the protractor below to find the measure of each angle.

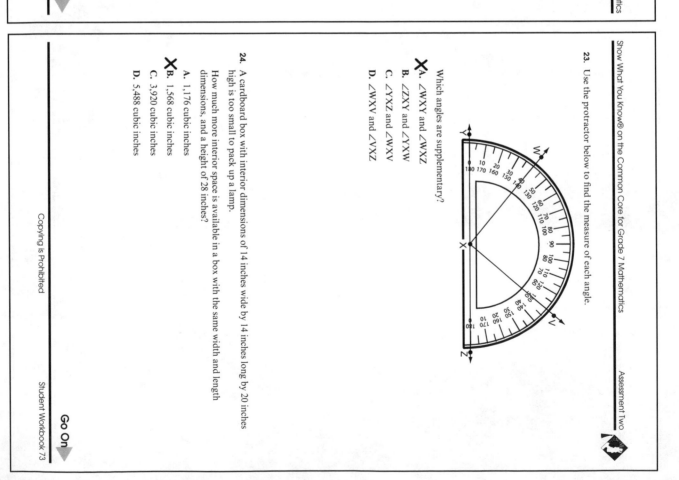

Which angles are supplementary?

✗ A. ∠WXY and ∠VXZ

   B. ∠ZXY and ∠YXW

   C. ∠YXZ and ∠WXV

   D. ∠WXV and ∠VXZ

24. A cardboard box with interior dimensions of 14 inches wide by 14 inches long by 20 inches high is too small to pack up a lamp.

How much more interior space is available in a box with the same width and length dimensions, and a height of 28 inches?

   A. 1,176 cubic inches

✗ B. 1,568 cubic inches

   C. 3,920 cubic inches

   D. 5,488 cubic inches

27. Shiny Bright Toy Company is having problems with quality control. Some customers have been complaining that parts are missing from their model car kits. Management decides to conduct a study to see how large the problem is. They randomly select 50 kits from one day's production and find that 3 of the kits are missing pieces.

If the factory normally produces 5,000 kits per day, how many are likely to be missing pieces?

A. 30

B. 50

✗ C. 300

D. 500

28. Compare the two sets of data from the Science Unit 1 Test scores in Mr. Walker's and Ms. Bernard's classes. The top possible score was 100%.

	Mr. Walker's Class	Ms. Bernard's Class
Range	76%	43%
Mean	52%	74%
Mode	61%	82%
Median	46%	78%

What conclusion can you draw about the test scores in Ms. Bernard's class?

A. The range indicates that most students in Ms. Bernard's class did not perform as well on the test, compared to those students in Mr. Walker's class.

B. The mean, median, and mode indicate that students in Mr. Walker's class performed better on the test than those in Ms. Bernard's class.

✗ C. The mean, median, and mode indicate that most students in Ms. Bernard's class performed better on the test than those in Mr. Walker's class.

D. The range indicates that most students in Mr. Walker's class performed better on the test than those in Ms. Bernard's class.

---

25. The state legislature has proposed instituting a "graduated license" for the state's teenaged drivers, which limits new teenaged drivers to daytime driving only. In addition, the restricted license limits new teenaged drivers to transport only one unrelated passenger under the age of 18. Ralph wants to conduct a survey to find out how much support there is for the proposed changes among the general public.

Which of the following would be the **best** way to conduct his survey?

A. Contact every resident of the state and ask each of them about the proposed changes.

B. Survey every member of the junior class in his high school.

C. Survey a random sample of the parents of all the students in his high school.

✗ D. Survey a random sample of all the registered voters in the state.

26. A scientist caught, tagged, and released back into a lake 75 trout. At the end of the next 30 days, the scientist caught 100 trout, 5 of which were tagged from the previous catch and release.

Which of the following would be the best estimate of the total trout population in this lake based only on the results of the research?

A. 750

✗ B. 1,500

C. 7,500

D. 12,750

29. Richard has a handful of jellybeans. There are 2 cherry, 4 lemon, and 3 grape.

    If he picks a jellybean at random, which flavor is **least** likely to be picked?

    ✗ A. cherry

    B. lemon

    C. grape

    D. all flavors are equally likely

30. A box of animal crackers has 8 different types of animals in it. Miranda takes 8 animal crackers out of the box and finds 3 lions.

    If the box of animal crackers has 32 crackers in it total, how many lions should Miranda expect to find in the box based on these results?

    A. 7 lions

    B. 9 lions

    ✗ C. 12 lions

    D. 18 lions

31. A regular deck of 52 cards has four suits: hearts, diamonds, spades, and clubs.

    What is the probability of drawing a diamond?

    A. 0

    ✗ B. $\frac{1}{4}$

    C. $\frac{1}{13}$

    D. $\frac{1}{52}$

32. Some friends were throwing rocks at a can. Each of the 4 friends threw 10 rocks. Jasper hit the can 5 times. Robin hit the can 9 times. Annie hit the can 6 times. Rodrigo hit the can 8 times.

    Based on these results, if Annie throws another rock, what is the probability that she will hit the can?

    A. $\frac{3}{20}$

    ✗ B. $\frac{3}{5}$

    C. $\frac{7}{11}$

    D. $\frac{7}{10}$

33. In a bag of mixed nuts, there are 28 peanuts, 14 cashews, 22 almonds, 10 walnuts, and 6 pecans.

    If 1 nut is taken from the bag without looking, what is the probability that a peanut will be selected?

    A. $\frac{7}{25}$

    B. $\frac{7}{13}$

    C. $\frac{13}{20}$

    ✗ D. $\frac{7}{20}$

---

35. The tree diagram below shows all possible gender combinations in a four-child family.

Possible Combinations of a Four-Child Family if Order Counts

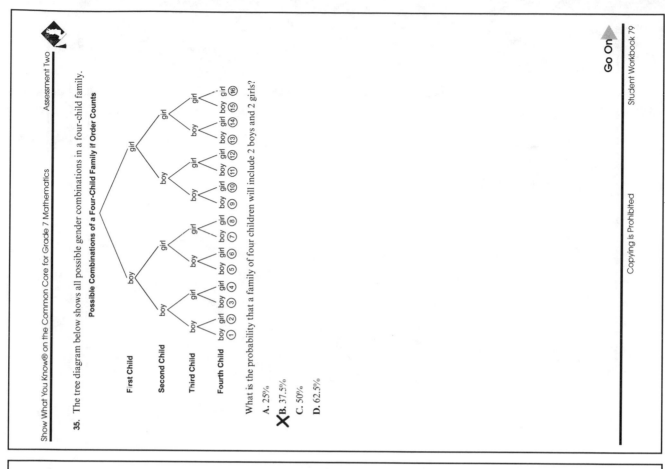

What is the probability that a family of four children will include 2 boys and 2 girls?

A. 25%

X **B.** 37.5%

C. 50%

D. 62.5%

Go On

---

34. Jim is making a banana split. He is going to use 3 scoops of ice cream. He has vanilla, chocolate, and strawberry to choose from.

How many different combinations of 3 scoops of ice cream does Jim have to choose from if the arrangement of the scoops does not matter?

A. 9 combinations

X **B.** 10 combinations

C. 18 combinations

D. 27 combinations

Go On

---

36. Look at the angles formed by the intersecting lines.

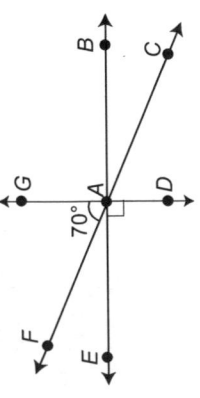

What is the measure of ∠BAC?

Show how you got your answer using words, numbers, or pictures.

Angle BAC has a degree measure of 20°.

Angles GAF and EAF are complementary angles because together they form a right angle and total 90°. Angle EAF must have a measure of 20° because of this relationship.

Angles EAF and BAC are vertical angles and therefore must have the same measure.

37. Five out of eight students in Mr. Hare's Science class have projects in the Science fair. Mr. Hare has a total of 152 students.

How many have projects in the Science fair?

A. 5
B. 40
C. 57
X D. 95

Go On

---

38. Azeem and Marian are playing their favorite board game. To play the game, they use two separate spinners. Spinner A is used to determine the number of cards they are dealt. Spinner B determines the number of spaces on the board the player gets to move his or her piece. For each player's turn, he or she must spin each spinner once. It's Marian's turn. She spins each spinner once.

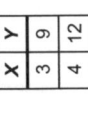

After spinning both spinners, how many possible pairs of outcomes are there?

A. 4
B. 7
X C. 12
D. 24

39. Simon created the following table.

X	Y
3	9
4	12
5	15
6	18

Does this table show a proportional relationship?

Explain your reasoning.

Yes, this does show a proportional relationship because each number in the y-column is a result of multiplying the "x" number by 3. In order for a proportional to be shown in a table like this, each number in the x-column would be multiplied by the same constant to produce the result in the y-column.

Go On

40. Look at the equation.

$$8 + -12 = \boxed{}$$

Which of these number lines represent this calculation?

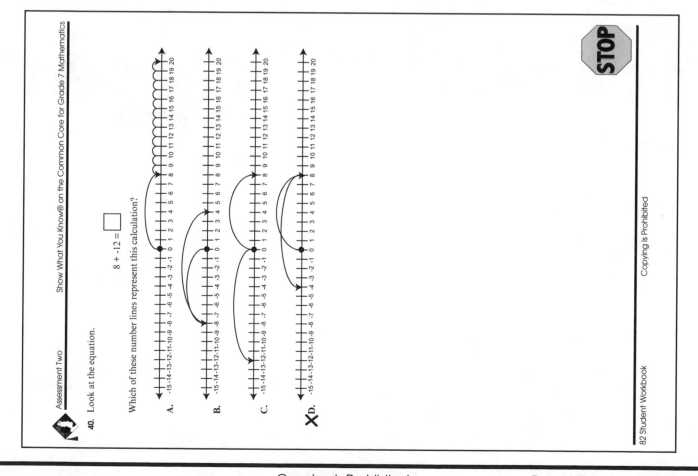

A.

B.

C.

X D.

1 Ⓐ Ⓑ ● Ⓓ

2 Ⓐ Ⓑ Ⓒ ●

3 Ⓐ ● Ⓒ Ⓓ

4 Ⓐ ● Ⓒ Ⓓ

5 Ⓐ Ⓑ ● Ⓓ

6 Ⓐ ● Ⓒ Ⓓ

7 Ⓐ ● Ⓒ Ⓓ

8

First convert the fraction 1/4 to a decimal, 0.25. Then multiply:
0.25 x 0.8 = 0.2.

$$\frac{1}{4} \times 0.8 = \underline{\quad 0.2 \quad\quad\quad\quad} .$$

9 Ⓐ ● Ⓒ Ⓓ

10 Ⓐ Ⓑ Ⓒ ●

11 Ⓐ ● Ⓒ Ⓓ

12 Ⓐ Ⓑ Ⓒ ●

13 Ⓐ Ⓑ Ⓒ ●

14

0.05(3 x $1.60 + 5 x $1.20 + $16.80) First find the cost of the notebooks by multiplying $1.60 by 3, then find the cost of the pencils by multiplying $1.20 by 5. Next add these two products to $16.80, the cost of the calculator, and multiply this total by 0.05, the decimal equivalent of 5%.
0.05(3 x $1.60 + 5 x $1.20 + $16.80) = 0.05($4.80 + $6.00 + $16.80) = 0.05($27.60) = $1.38. Saleem pays $1.38 in sales tax.

Total sales tax = _____$1.38_____ .

15 Ⓐ Ⓑ ● Ⓓ

16 ● Ⓑ Ⓒ Ⓓ

17 ● Ⓑ Ⓒ Ⓓ

18

A trapezoid is a figure that has two acute angles and two obtuse angles, as shown in the figure below.

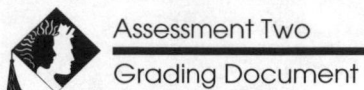

19 Ⓐ ● Ⓒ Ⓓ

20 Ⓐ Ⓑ ● Ⓓ

21 Ⓐ Ⓑ ● Ⓓ

22

In this case, when solving, it is easier to use the fraction form of π.
So, $44 = d(22/7)$; $308 = 22d$; $d = 14$.

The value of the circle's diameter is ____14____ .

23 ● Ⓑ Ⓒ Ⓓ

24 Ⓐ ● Ⓒ Ⓓ

25 Ⓐ Ⓑ Ⓒ ●

26 Ⓐ ● Ⓒ Ⓓ

27 Ⓐ Ⓑ ● Ⓓ

28 Ⓐ Ⓑ ● Ⓓ

29 ● Ⓑ Ⓒ Ⓓ

30 Ⓐ Ⓑ ● Ⓓ

31 Ⓐ ● Ⓒ Ⓓ

32 Ⓐ ● Ⓒ Ⓓ

33 Ⓐ Ⓑ Ⓒ ●

34 Ⓐ ● Ⓒ Ⓓ

35 Ⓐ ● Ⓒ Ⓓ

36

Angle BAC has a degree measure of 20°.

Angles GAF and EAF are complementary angles because together they form a right angle and total 90°. Angle EAF must have a measure of 20° because of this relationship.

Angles EAF and BAC are vertical angles and therefore must have the same measure.

∠BAC = ___20°_____ .

37 Ⓐ Ⓑ Ⓒ ⬤

38 Ⓐ Ⓑ ⬤ Ⓓ

39

Yes, this does show a proportional relationship because each number in the *y*-column is a result of multiplying the "*x*" number by 3. In order for a proportional relationship to be shown in a table like this, each number in the *x*-column would be multiplied by the same constant to produce the result in the *y*-column.

40 Ⓐ Ⓑ Ⓒ ⬤

Question	Standard	Answer	Keywords
1	7.RP.1	C	Unit Rate, Fraction
2	7.RP.2	D	Proportion, Direct Variation
3	7.RP.2	B	Proportion, Equation, Table
4	7.RP.3	B	Percent
5	7.RP.3	C	Percent
6	7.NS.1	B	Integers, Subtraction
7	7.NS.2	B	Integers, Division
8	7.NS.2	—	Fraction, Decimal, Rational Numbers, Division
9	7.NS.2	B	Rational Numbers, Multiplication, Integers, Fractions
10	7.NS.3	D	Integers
11	7.EE.1	B	Simplify, Algebraic Expression
12	7.EE.2	D	Percent, Equation
13	7.EE.3	D	Percent, Sales Tax
14	7.EE.3	—	Percent, Sales Tax, Multi-Step
15	7.EE.4	C	Write Equation
16	7.EE.4	A	Solve Equations, Volume
17	7.G.1	A	Scale Drawing, Proportions
18	7.G.2	—	Geometric Figures, Draw, Trapezoid
19	7.G.3	B	Cross-Section, Three-Dimensional
20	7.G.4	C	Circumference, Circle

—see analysis for constructed response

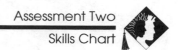

Question	Standard	Answer	Keywords
21	7.G.4	C	Area, Circle
22	7.G.4	—	Circumference, Circle
23	7.G.5	A	Supplementary, Angle Measurement
24	7.G.6	B	Volume, Rectangular Prism
25	7.SP.1	D	Sample, Statistics
26	7.SP.2	B	Sampling, Population Size
27	7.SP.2	C	Sampling, Prediction
28	7.SP.4	C	Median, Compare Data, Mean, Mode
29	7.SP.5	A	Probability, Likelihood of Events
30	7.SP.6	C	Probability, Prediction
31	7.SP.7	B	Probability, Simple Event
32	7.SP.7	B	Probability, Simple Event
33	7.SP.7	D	Probability, Simple Event
34	7.SP.8	B	Sample Space, Outcomes
35	7.SP.8	B	Probability, Compound Events
36	7.G.5	—	Complementary, Vertical Angles, Angle Measurement
37	7.RP.3	D	Proportions
38	7.SP.8	C	Sample Space, Outcomes
39	7.RP.2	—	Proportion, Table
40	7.NS.1	D	Integers, Addition

—see analysis for constructed response

Mathematics Assessment Two: Correlation Chart

Use this chart to identify areas for improvement for individual students or for the class as a whole. For example, enter students' names in the left-hand column. When a student misses a question, place an "X" in the corresponding box. A column with a large number of "Xs" shows that the class needs more practice with that particular objective.

Correlation	7.RP.1	7.RP.2	7.RP.2	7.RP.3	7.RP.3	7.NS.1	7.NS.2	7.NS.2	7.NS.2	7.NS.3	7.EE.1	7.EE.2	7.EE.3	7.EE.3	7.EE.4	7.EE.4	7.G.1	7.G.2	7.G.3	7.G.4
Answer	C	D	B	B	C	B	B	—	B	D	B	D	D	—	C	A	A	—	B	C
Question	1	2	3	4	5	6	7	8	9	10	11	12	13	14	15	16	17	18	19	20

Student Names

—*see analysis for constructed response*

	Correlation	7.G.4	7.G.4	7.G.5	7.G.6	7.SP.1	7.SP.2	7.SP.2	7.SP.4	7.SP.5	7.SP.6	7.SP.7	7.SP.7	7.SP.7	7.SP.8	7.SP.8	7.G.5	7.RP.3	7.SP.8	7.RP.2	7.NS.1
	Answer	C	—	A	B	D	B	C	C	A	C	B	B	D	B	B	—	D	C	—	D
	Question	21	22	23	24	25	26	27	28	29	30	31	32	33	34	35	36	37	38	39	40
Student Names																					

—see analysis for constructed response

Show What You Know® on the COMMON CORE

Assessing Student Knowledge of the Common Core State Standards (CCSS)
Reading • Mathematics • Grades 3–8

Diagnostic Test-Preparation Student Workbooks and Parent/Teacher Editions for Grades 3–5

Single Subject Student Workbooks and Parent/Teacher Editions for Grades 6–8

For more information, call our toll-free number: 1.877.PASSING (727.7464)
or visit our website: www.showwhatyouknowpublishing.com